The Great Chicago Fire

The Great Chicago Fire

Dynise Balcavage

CHELSEA HOUSE PUBLISHERS
Philadelphia

Frontispiece: The Great Fire of 1871
envelopes Chicago in flames.

CHELSEA HOUSE PUBLISHERS

Editor in Chief Sally Cheney
Associate Editor in Chief Kim Shinners
Production Manager Pamela Loos
Art Director Sara Davis
Director of Photography Judy L. Hasday

Staff for THE GREAT CHICAGO FIRE

Senior Editor LeeAnne Gelletly
Assistant Editor Brian Baughan
Associate Art Director/Designer Takeshi Takahashi
Picture Researcher Patricia Burns
Cover Designer Takeshi Takahashi

First Printing

1 3 5 7 9 8 6 4 2

The Chelsea House World Wide Web address is
http://www.chelseahouse.com

Library of Congress Cataloging-in-Publication Data

Balcavage, Dynise.
The Great Chicago Fire / Dynise Balcavage.
    p. cm. — (Great disasters, reforms and ramifications)
Includes bibliographical references and index.

ISBN 0-7910-5269-9 (alk. paper)

1. Fires—Illinois—Chicago—History—19th century—
Juvenile literature. 2. Chicago (Ill.)—History—To 1875—
Juvenile literature. [I. Fires—Illinois—Chicago—History—
19th century. 2. Chicago (Ill.)—History—To 1875.]
I. Title II. Series.

F548.42.B22 2001
977.3'11041—dc21

                                        2001028283

Contents

GREAT DISASTERS
REFORMS and RAMIFICATIONS

Jill McCaffrey
National Chairman
Armed Forces Emergency Services
American Red Cross

Introduction

Disasters have always been a source of fascination and awe. Tales of a great flood that nearly wipes out all life are among humanity's oldest recorded stories, dating at least from the second millennium B.C., and they appear in cultures from the Middle East to the Arctic Circle to the southernmost tip of South America and the islands of Polynesia. Typically gods are at the center of these ancient disaster tales—which is perhaps not too surprising, given the fact that the tales originated during a time when human beings were at the mercy of natural forces they did not understand.

To a great extent, we still are at the mercy of nature, as anyone who reads the newspapers or watches nightly news broadcasts can attest.

Hurricanes, earthquakes, tornados, wildfires, and floods continue to exact a heavy toll in suffering and death, despite our considerable knowledge of the workings of the physical world. If science has offered only limited protection from the consequences of natural disasters, it has in no way diminished our fascination with them. Perhaps that's because the scale and power of natural disasters force us as individuals to confront our relatively insignificant place in the physical world and remind us of the fragility and transience of our lives. Perhaps it's because we can imagine ourselves in the midst of dire circumstances and wonder how we would respond. Perhaps it's because disasters seem to bring out the best and worst instincts of humanity: altruism and selfishness, courage and cowardice, generosity and greed.

As one of the national chairmen of the American Red Cross, a humanitarian organization that provides relief for victims of disasters, I have had the privilege of seeing some of humanity's best instincts. I have witnessed communities pulling together in the face of trauma; I have seen thousands of people answer the call to help total strangers in their time of need.

Of course, helping victims after a tragedy is not the only way, or even the best way, to deal with disaster. In many cases planning and preparation can minimize damage and loss of life—or even avoid a disaster entirely. For, as history repeatedly shows, many disasters are caused not by nature but by human folly, shortsightedness, and unethical conduct. For example, when a land developer wanted to create a lake for his exclusive resort club in Pennsylvania's Allegheny Mountains in 1880, he ignored expert warnings and cut corners in reconstructing an earthen dam. On May 31, 1889, the dam gave way, unleashing 20 million tons of water on the towns below. The Johnstown Flood, the deadliest in American history, claimed more than 2,200 lives. Greed and negligence would figure prominently in the Triangle Shirtwaist Company fire in 1911. Deplorable conditions in the garment sweatshop, along with a failure to give any thought to the safety of workers, led to the tragic deaths of 146 persons. Technology outstripped wisdom only a year later, when the designers of the luxury liner *Titanic* smugly declared their state-of-the-art ship "unsinkable," seeing no need to provide lifeboat capacity for everyone onboard. On the night of April 14, 1912, more than 1,500 passengers and crew paid for this hubris with their lives after the ship collided with an iceberg and sank. But human catastrophes aren't always the unforeseen consequences of carelessness or folly. In the 1940s the leaders of Nazi Germany purposefully and systematically set out to exterminate all Jews, along with Gypsies, homosexuals, the mentally ill, and other so-called undesirables. More recently terrorists have targeted random members of society, blowing up airplanes and buildings in an effort to advance their political agendas.

The books in the GREAT DISASTERS: REFORMS AND RAMIFICATIONS series examine these and other famous disasters, natural and human made. They explain the causes of the disasters, describe in detail how events unfolded, and paint vivid portraits of the people caught up in dangerous circumstances. But these books are more than just accounts of what happened to whom and why. For they place the disasters in historical perspective, showing how people's attitudes and actions changed and detailing the steps society took in the wake of each calamity. And in the end, the most important lesson we can learn from any disaster—as well as the most fitting tribute to those who suffered and died—is how to avoid a repeat in the future.

A Recipe
for Disaster

In 1871 much of Chicago was a closely built collection of wooden cottages, tenement buildings, and factories. The branches of the Chicago River separated the city into three main geographical sections, referred to at the time as the North Division (right), the South Division (left), and the West Division (top).

Late on the Saturday evening of October 7, 1871, the insistent clanging of alarm bells jarred Chicago city firefighters from their sleep. Sometime after 10 P.M. a blaze had broken out in the boiler room of the Lull and Holmes planing mill, a woodworking shop located at 209 South Canal Street in the West Division of the city.

Fires had become fairly commonplace in 19th-century Chicago. The city's newly installed fire-alarm system had been put to the test frequently that summer, one of Chicago's driest ever. From Independence Day to October 7 barely an inch and a half of rain had fallen. Carelessly handled lanterns and dropped candles in hay-filled wooden barns ignited blazes quickly fueled by the southwesterly winds sweeping off the prairie. Fires had become such everyday events—about 20 per week—that city

11

residents had come to ignore the deep-toned peals of the Cook County Courthouse bell as it warned of yet another fire.

Although Chicago had averaged about two fires each day the previous year, city officials had not addressed the need for improving its fire department. The city's 334,000 residents relied on the protection of only 185 firemen, who were equipped with just 17 horse-drawn steam engines, 6 hose carts, 4 hook and ladder trucks, and 2 hose elevators.

Now once again Chicago firefighters were being called into action as the alarm tolled over the darkened city. The firemen jumped into their horse-drawn steam pumpers and hose carts and sped off to Canal Street, where ominous flames leaped wildly into the black night sky, threatening to race through the West Division. But the men fought back—along with hundreds of volunteers—hauling heavy canvas hoses and pumping streams of water onto the fiery blaze. Determined to stop the flames from spreading, firefighters struggled in the heat and swirling, smoky haze as the fire grew into one of the worst blazes ever to hit Chicago.

And stop it they did, although the weary firefighters did not extinguish the last of the glowing embers until early the next afternoon. Chicago's fire department battled for 16 hours in its effort to prevent a large-scale catastrophe. Still, before the Canal Street blaze was put out, it had destroyed four city blocks (about 16 acres of land) and caused about $1 million of damage.

The 16-hour battle took its toll on Chicago's woefully understaffed fire department. Of its 185 members, about 60 suffered from burns and smoke inhalation. Some had to be sent home, injured or suffering from blistered skin, swollen eyelids, and smoke-congested lungs. The rest, although exhausted and ill, straggled back to their company firehouses, anxious to grab some much needed sleep. Fighting the immense blaze had taken a tremendous effort. By the afternoon of Sunday, October 8, 1871, no one in Chicago's fire department was in shape to fight any more fires that day.

*   *   *

In October 1871 the booming Midwestern town of Chicago, Illinois, claimed the title of the fastest-growing city in the world. Located along Lake Michigan at the mouth of the Chicago River, the city bridged the industrial East with the agricultural West. People, money, and goods flowed in and out of the bustling metropolis, aptly dubbed the Queen of the West.

Chicago residents boasted with pride of their industrial, commercial, and cultural center. Ten railroads running between the East and West Coasts made the city their hub. Chicago housed thousands of factories and grocery, retail, wholesale, and department stores. Seventeen grain elevators that could store up to 12 million bushels clustered along the Chicago River beside countless stockyards. The biggest of these slaughterhouses, Union Stock Yard, had processed more than 3 million head of livestock that year. Since the mid-1800s the booming city had been attracting a multitude of immigrants hoping to share in Chicago's prosperity.

Just 100 years earlier the Chicago area had been nothing more than a combination of swampland and prairie, sparsely inhabited by several clans of Native Americans. It was a peaceful place then, overflowing with nature's majestic beauty, unspoiled by the shovels and pickaxes of men. The waterways of the region provided transportation for the Native Americans, who could easily portage (carry over land) their canoes from the Des Plaines River to the Chicago River and paddle on from there to Lake Michigan.

Few people actually lived in the area because of its swampy, wet marshlands. But the Potawatomi Indians gave the place a name: "Chicago," which is most likely derived from the Potawatomi word *checaugou*. It translates roughly to "wild onions" or "cabbage"; at the time, skunk cabbage and wild onions could be found growing wild and in abundance throughout the swampy area.

French explorers were the first non-Indians to frequent the place. The famous frontiersmen Jacques Marquette and Louis Jolliet, best known for their exploration of the Mississippi River, in all likelihood passed through Chicago in 1673. However, the first non-Indian settler was Jean Baptiste Point du Sable. The French-African fur trader from New Orleans, Louisiana, probably understood and undoubtedly profited from the advantageous location of Chicago, which served as a crossroads between the Canadian fur traders and the buyers from the United States.

Around 1779 du Sable founded the first permanent settlement at the mouth of the Chicago River in what is now downtown Chicago. There he, his Potawatomi wife, and their three children opened the first trading post in what was eventually to become one of America's busiest and biggest cities.

About 20 years later the U.S. government recognized that the region served as an important portage area connecting the East, West, and South. Consequently, in 1803 the U.S. Army oversaw the construction of Fort Dearborn, a small fort strategically located at the mouth of the Chicago River. The fort was destroyed soon afterwards, during the War of 1812 in a battle against Native Americans who had allied themselves with the British. But the U.S. Army reconstructed it four years later. Once Fort Dearborn was rebuilt, settlers returned to the area again and began to set up residence.

In 1833 the muddy trading post of Chicago, with its 43 houses and 200 citizens, was incorporated as a village. By then only a small number of Native Americans were left in the area. As of the late 1830s the city had established its first schools, theaters, and businesses, and soon afterward, with a population of more than 4,000, it was incorporated as a city.

The new city grew quickly. By 1844 its population had nearly doubled. Many businesses—especially manufacturing and food processing factories—set up shop in Chicago, aided by the growth of railroads, which by 1853 had made the city a primary terminal. Immigrants from all over the world flocked to Chicago, often by railroad. On a single day in 1857, more than 34,000 immigrants arrived at Chicago by train from New York, lured by the rumors of abundant work.

The city's population had grown tremendously since the 1850s, mostly due to the large influx of European immigrants, such as this group of Dutch settlers, seeking homes in the Midwest. Over the years, thousands of newcomers traveled by train to the city in search of jobs.

By 1870 about half of Chicago's population of more than 300,000 had been born in countries other than America. The largest numbers of foreign-born Chicago residents were Germans, followed by the Irish, Bohemians, and Scandinavians. Families tended to cluster by nationality within their own neighborhoods, where they could speak the language of their homeland and carry on their traditional customs.

Chicago's lakefront location and access to the Chicago River ensured its position as a city of commerce, from its early days as a trading post to its status in 1871 as a booming, industrialized town. Almost 60,000 buildings filled the six-by-three-mile area that made up Chicago, which was in turn divided by the branches of the Chicago River into three distinct sections, known as the South, North, and West Divisions.

The South Division contained the central business district, which featured many of the city's grand hotels, banks, theaters, and stores. This same area boasted the mansions of the well-to-do who frequented the business district, but it also included neighborhoods where the much poorer residents lived. One of these sections was the Irish immigrant shantytown known as Conley's Patch, referred to in the *Chicago Tribune* as "the most squalid, poverty-stricken, crime-stained portion of Chicago"; it consisted mostly of run-down hovels and tenements.

West of the south branch of the Chicago River lay the West Division. Here many of Chicago's middle class and poor owned or rented cottages. Most of these neighborhoods were built immediately adjacent to commercial areas containing factories, lumberyards, wood mills, coal distributors, and furniture makers. Irish immigrants like Patrick O'Leary, a Civil War veteran, his wife,

Catherine, and their five children made their home in the West Division.

In the North Division stood the expensive stone-and-brick homes of Chicago's oldest and most prestigious families, as well as the ostentatious mansions of Chicago's newly rich. Scattered amidst the opulent homes of millionaire families like the Gordon Hubbards, the George Rumseys, and the William Ogdens were the modest wood-frame cottages of German and Scandinavian immigrant workers.

As in most cities, certain buildings in Chicago stood out as landmarks in their neighborhoods, easily recognized as symbols of the city's prosperity. One of the best known—the Cook County Courthouse—stood in the South Division. Constructed of limestone and topped by

Two well-known landmarks of the city's North Division resembled small limestone castles. Operational since 1869, the waterworks (background) housed the pumping station that distributed water throughout the city by underground pipes. One of Chicago's tallest structures, the water tower (center) contained a 138-foot standpipe used to equalize water pressure.

a wooden cupola containing a 7,200-pound bell, the courthouse cost more than $1 million to build. The large, ornately decorated building, surrounded by 10 spacious acres in the central business district, housed most of the city and county government offices. All public papers and records of titles to real estate in Cook County were stored at the courthouse. Its basement contained the local jail.

The elegantly constructed courthouse building impressed Chicago residents and visitors alike. But of more importance than its architecture was the enormous bell mounted in its cupola. In his newspaper feature "Bygone Days in Chicago," *Chicago Times* reporter Frederick Francis Cook described how the ringing of this bell affected the citizens' everyday lives: "In a way . . . the Court House was everybody's monitor and guide. It told you when to rise, when to eat your dinner, when to knock off work, when to jubilate, when to mourn, and, above all, it helped you to locate fires; for the clang of its great bell would be heard in almost every part of the town."

Two other famous city landmarks, located on North Michigan Avenue in the North Division, were the Chicago Water Tower and Waterworks. Built in a Gothic style—complete with towers, pointed arches, and vaulted ceilings—the two buildings consisted of large limestone blocks that had been quarried in nearby Joliet, Illinois. The waterworks contained four powerful pumping engines that distributed water throughout the city through an innovative pumping system that had begun operation just two years earlier, in 1869.

Although many of Chicago's grand landmarks were constructed of limestone, like the courthouse and waterworks, most of the rest of Chicago had been built of wood—the building material of choice in the city, where

timber was abundant, cheap, and relatively easy to obtain. Numerous wood mills and factories lined the south branch of the Chicago River, their lumberyards containing veritable mountains of wood, ready to be made into structures.

Even the roads and sidewalks of the city were made of wood. Because the town had been built on swampland, heavy rains often reduced its unpaved streets to mud, which made walking or driving a carriage difficult at worst and messy at best. Most of Chicago's mud-filled streets were not much higher than nearby Lake Michigan, and they seldom dried out. Their open sewers also created many health problems. However, resourceful Chicagoans made some of the roads passable, regardless of the weather, by paving them with wood. By 1871 the city contained 57 miles of wood-paved streets and 561 miles of raised wooden sidewalks.

Clark Street in early Chicago. As the city grew, residents made muddy roads passable by paving them with planks and building raised wooden sidewalks. By 1871 Chicago contained more than 600 miles of these flammable streets and walkways.

About two-thirds of Chicago's buildings—its houses, churches, stores, and factories—were crafted of timber as well. Even many grand structures that appeared to be built of stone or brick often proved to be little more than wooden frames covered with masonry facades. Supposedly fireproof structures that had been crafted of fire-resistant materials, such as marble or brick, sported highly flammable wooden signs or ornamentation or had wood-framed, tar-covered roofs. Many of the so-called stone-carved facades or marble fronts decorating Chicago's buildings were actually nothing more than painted wood.

Early Chicago had few building codes, so residents— rich or poor—could build homes or businesses in any fashion they chose. Rambling wooden additions filled the small lots of the city's poorer families. Wealthier citizens chose brick and stone to embellish the exteriors of their well-appointed homes. However, this ornamentation was largely just for show; the mansions, by and large, were crafted from the ubiquitous wood.

Members of Chicago's fire department believed that far too many of the city's buildings were poorly and dangerously built, often by "swindling" builders. In a report presented to the mayor and city council, the department had expressed concern over "the grave defects of the manner in which our city [is] being built." A *Chicago Tribune* editorial published on September 1, 1871, criticized the new, poorly built constructions, calling them "miles of fire traps, pleasing to the eye, looking substantial, but all shams and shingles." Some people worried that all of these poorly built wooden structures in the city created a dangerous fire hazard.

Concerned about the situation, officials in the Chicago Fire Department pushed for fire safety reforms.

Unfortunately, the enforcement of these requested building codes and rules would have required raising citizens' taxes—an unpopular action.

Still, chief fire marshal Robert A. Williams persisted in his quest to institute new reforms. The fire department repeatedly asked that a building inspection code be established, that hotels and large public buildings be required to have metal roofs, and that more fire hydrants and water mains be installed throughout the city. Williams also recommended that Chicago hire more personnel for the fire department and buy two fireboats with water pumps to patrol the river, which itself was lined with lumberyards and spanned by wooden bridges. Officials in the city government, however, rejected each request, arguing that the resulting higher taxes would discourage the city's growth.

The Chicago Fire Department had some of the most up-to-date firefighting equipment, such as the steam engine *R. A. Williams*, which had a boiler, engine, and pump. But the organization was seriously understaffed, with just 185 men serving a community of 330,000.

Nevertheless, the city did make a few improvements. In 1871 Chicago installed a fire alarm system that at the time was considered one of the best in the nation.

From firehouse observation decks watchmen scanned the neighborhoods—the highest observation post was the wooden cupola of the Cook County Courthouse, which stood 100 feet above the ground. When someone spotted a fire, he or she could report it by telegraph from the local fire station or from one of the 172 numbered alarm boxes located on the outside of buildings throughout the city. The boxes were locked to prevent tricksters from pulling false alarms, and the keys were entrusted only to citizens in local residences and owners of businesses who were considered responsible. Once an alarm was received at the central alarm station in the Cook County Courthouse, the watchman there would strike the appropriately numbered alarm box. This action rang the massive bell in the courthouse cupola and telegraphed the fire's location to the station of the closest fire department company.

Throughout that scorching summer of 1871 city residents became accustomed to hearing the tolls of that courthouse bell, warning of more and more fires. As the hot, dry months passed with little rain, Chicagoans watched their tar-covered roofs soften in the blazing sun and saw the drought-stricken trees lining the streets lose their leaves as early as July.

By autumn, dry winds had scattered the parched trees' brittle leaves, blowing them into dusty piles in alleyways. At the same time, residents were carelessly storing stove kindling and wood shavings beneath their houses or in their yards. Some families prepared for winter by hoarding hay in their barns to feed their livestock and wood in sheds to heat their homes. In the basements of the wealthy, families stockpiled large supplies of kerosene and coal for use during the coming winter.

The entire city was a tinderbox, ready to burn. An editorial in the October 8 issue of the *Chicago Tribune* warned that "the absence of rain for three weeks [has] left everything in so flammable a condition that a spark might set a fire which would sweep from end to end of the city." Little did the *Tribune* editors guess how accurate—and timely—this prediction would be.

On October 7, Chicago city firefighters managed to prevent a catastrophic fire when they contained the 16-hour-long blaze that enveloped Canal Street, although the flames did cause extensive damage. But the Saturday-night fire depleted the number of men in an already understaffed fire department, as many were left exhausted and injured.

The city's firefighting equipment fared poorly as well. The extensive blaze damaged two fire engines—the *William James* Engine No. 3 and the *Liberty* Engine No. 7, leaving both in need of repair. Another engine, *Chicago* Engine No. 5, was damaged but still usable. One of the city's four hook and ladder wagons was completely destroyed, and canvas hoses, burned up by the Canal Street blaze, were in short supply.

It was the worst possible time for another fire, for virtually all of Chicago's defenses were down.

City on Fire

Through a series of mishaps the small blaze that originated in the West Division on De Koven Street exploded into a massive conflagration. Within just a few hours it reached the wood mills, furniture factories, and grain elevators that lined the shore of the south branch of the Chicago River.

A warm breeze blew through the city of Chicago the Sunday evening of October 8. At around nine o'clock 40-year-old fire watchman Mathias Schaffer was giving some visitors a tour of his observation post in the Cook County Courthouse tower when one of Schaffer's visitors pointed out gray plumes of smoke to the southwest. At first glance the watchman believed that the haze was due to the smoldering ashes of Saturday night's Canal Street blaze. Soon afterward Schaffer scanned the area again, this time with his spyglass. He was startled to see the haze had become flames, glowing brightly against the dark night sky.

The watchman then realized that this was a new fire, near the Canal Street blaze of the day before. Schaffer quickly calculated that the flames were coming from the intersection of Canalport Avenue and Halsted

Street. From atop the courthouse he reported the fire's location through the voice tube (similar to an intercom system) to his assistant, telegraph operator William J. Brown. The young man worked on the third floor of the central fire-alarm telegraph office as the night operator.

Schaffer told Brown to strike alarm code box 342. This would ring the courthouse bell and the alarm in the firehouse located nearest to the fire. At approximately 9:30 P.M., as the bell rang its stern warning over a sleepy Chicago, exhausted firemen from the station for code box 342 set off to tame yet another blaze.

Just a few minutes later, however, Schaffer realized he had incorrectly guessed the fire's position by about a mile. He frantically called down to Brown, telling him to ring alarm box 319, which was closer to the correct location of the blaze. But Brown adamantly refused to send the new directions, explaining that the change would confuse the firefighters. He convinced Schaffer that the engine company would pass by the flames on its way to alarm box 342 and reroute anyway.

This new fire had originated at 137 De Koven Street, near the home of Irish immigrant Patrick O'Leary. According to a neighbor, Daniel "Peg Leg" Sullivan, he first spotted the flames shooting out from the O'Leary's barn, which stood behind the family cottage. Catherine O'Leary ran a milk business from the building, which housed five cows, a calf, and a horse.

At about 8:45 P.M. Sullivan's frantic calls had alerted the neighborhood to the fire. Seeing that the O'Leary barn was ablaze, he later explained, he entered it to save some of the livestock inside. However, the barn and an adjacent shed were filled with about two tons of hay, coal, and firewood—all of which fed the greedy flames—and the fire spread quickly. Nearby resident Dennis Rogan heard Sullivan's cries and woke the

O'Leary family, whose members had already gone to bed. They and their neighbors tried to save the O'Leary cottage and contain the fire.

At around nine o'clock another neighbor, William Lee, ran three and a half blocks to Goll's Drugstore, whose shopkeeper had a key for the fire alarm box hanging on the outside of his store. Lee would later claim that Goll had not allowed him to turn in the alarm. Goll would counter that he himself turned in two alarms. In what was one more event in a series of misfortunes, however, the call did not register at the central alarm office in the county courthouse.

Among the crowd of spectators who were drawn to the growing blaze was Joseph E. Chamberlain, a 20-year-old reporter for the *Chicago Evening Post*. "I was at the scene in a few minutes," Chamberlain later reported. "The fire had already advanced a distance of about a single square through the frame buildings that covered the ground thickly north of De Koven Street and east of Jefferson Street."

While the flames spread, Schaffer's incorrect directions delayed the arrival of the fire department. Eventually, firemen on the horse-drawn steam engine *America* managed to spot the fire on De Koven Street, which was just a few minutes from the area that had been burned the night before. The *America* sped to the blaze, with a second fire engine, the *Little Giant*, not far behind.

Unfortunately, by the time the other fire engines found the fire, the flames had spread too far to be easily controlled. And some fire companies did not prove very useful either. *Chicago* Engine No. 5 broke down shortly after arriving and was unable to pump water right away. Meanwhile, the fire grew, as powerful flames raced through dozens of flimsy one-story wooden buildings, cow sheds, and corn cribs. The southwesterly winds blowing off of the prairie helped push the blaze onward to the east and north.

Within an hour of receiving the alarm, seven fire companies had managed to arrive on the scene. There chief fire marshal Robert A. Williams frantically tried to position his engines and firemen in the best locations to battle the spreading blaze, directing the engines to encircle the burning neighborhoods. The firefighters worked feverishly, trying to contain the growing inferno. Groups of two would lug their heavy canvas hose as close to the fire as possible, then together hold the hose in a steady aim at the flames. As the water struck hot wood, it emitted a tremendous blast of smoke and steam. The intense heat singed the hair on the men's heads and arms, blinded their eyes, and even made their clothes smolder.

Seeing how quickly the fire was spreading, one firefighter tried to send in a second alarm—a call for additional engines and personnel—from the alarm box at Goll's Drugstore. However, he neglected to use the correct signal of pulling the lever four times, which indicated a second alarm. Although the signal from the drugstore alarm box registered back at the courthouse, neither Mathias Schaffer nor William Brown understood it was a call for more help. Both assumed someone was reporting the fire they had already seen, and to which they had already sent fire engines.

Back at De Koven a loud, rowdy crowd of men and boys had quickly gathered almost as soon as the fire first started. Although blazes were common in the city, they still provided a form of entertainment for its residents. Many of these curious spectators had come over the bridge from Chicago's South Division, where they lived in Conley's Patch, an Irish immigrant community just across the southern branch of the Chicago River. Some in

A firefighter struggles to carry a bulky fire hose. Unlike the city's steam engines, the hose carts could not throw water very far. To fight a blaze effectively, firemen using hose carts had to stand close to flames, enduring furnacelike blasts of heat and smoke.

the group were so drunk and boisterous that the firemen had to spray them with water in order to quiet them down.

Indeed, the fire must have been a tremendous sight—the dry, southwesterly winds had begun to whip fiercely, making the flames leap as high as 500 feet in the air. As firemen kept trying desperately to stop the blaze from spreading, wind gusts blew flaming firebrands over the men's heads. New blazes quickly started wherever the fiery pieces of wood landed. Sparks and glowing embers fell like red rain, lighting up the night sky and casting an eerie orange glow on the spectators' faces.

Police officers and citizens joined the firemen in defending their city. Although they managed to keep the fire from moving west, they could do nothing about the blaze's insolent push to the northeast, toward the nearby industrial district of lumberyards, wooden warehouses, and stores of coal.

From his lookout at the Cook County Courthouse, young William Brown could see that the blaze was continuing to grow. So he decided to signal a second alarm, this time without Schaffer's approval. But once more he transmitted the wrong box number, and again, backup fire engines sped off to yet another fire that did not exist.

By 10:00 P.M. the fire had spread five blocks north to the steeple of St. Paul's Church, which quickly ignited when fiery missiles from the blaze landed on its roof. Once the furniture-finishing factory next door to the church caught fire, there was little more to be done to stop the flames' steady northward advance.

At 10:30 P.M. Brown sent a third alarm, and again he keyed in the incorrect box number. But this time it wasn't a grave mistake. By now, the conflagration was so out of control and so gargantuan that it lit up the sky. No one could miss it.

In another hour the numerous wood mills and furniture factories that lined the river were ablaze. Grain elevators began burning from the top down. When the fire eventually reached the Canal Street neighborhood that had burned the night before, fire officials breathed a sigh of relief. Here, they hoped, where the buildings had already burned to the ground, the flames surely would stop, since so little was left there to catch fire. But they were wrong. At this point the fire was so powerful that the dry winds easily propelled the flames onward.

A dramatic account published later by the *Chicago Post* described the awesome scene:

The earth and sky were fire and flames; the atmosphere was smoke. A perfect hurricane was blowing, and drew the fiery billows with a screech through the narrow alleys between the tall buildings as if it were sucking them through a tube; great sheets of flames literally flapped in the air like sails on shipboard. . . . Roofing became detached in great sheets, and drove down the sky like huge, blazing arrows. The dust and smoke filled one's eyes and nostrils with bitter and irritating clouds.

At half past eleven a fiery ball from the West Division fire flew across the south branch of the Chicago River, landing on the horse stable roof of the Parmelee Omnibus and Stage Company. The blaze had leaped

Both firefighters and citizens joined forces to battle the blaze, but strong winds flung flaming brands over their heads, igniting the rooftops of nearby buildings. Nothing could stop the flames from spreading.

across the water from the West Division to establish its first stronghold in the South Division of Chicago. The 50-yard-wide river had presented no barrier to the blaze.

A Chicago reporter telegraphed a graphic description of the fire's early progress to the *San Francisco Morning Bulletin*, which printed the following article Monday morning:

> Chicago, Oct. 9–1:15 A.M. — The fire is still raging and with increased fury. It has spread almost with the velocity of the wind, and has now reached West Monroe street, a distance [of] more than a mile from where it started, and it covers a breadth of nearly half a mile reaching from the river to Jefferson street. The district already burned over involves an immense number of lumber yards, and the freight depots of the Chicago, St. Louis, and Pittsburgh, Fort Wayne and Chicago roads. The property already destroyed counts up many millions of dollars, and perhaps the half is not told.
>
> The task of [stopping the blaze] seems fourfold greater than it did one hour ago, and none dare venture the opinion as to when or where it will stop. Brands from the fire were blown across to the east side of the river and set a wooden building on fire directly adjoining the Chicago gas house. The flames spread in every direction, the adjoining buildings being all of the tinder box kind, the prospect is that the gas house will be destroyed and the city draped in darkness. A terrible panic is prevailing throughout the whole city. Almost everybody

The telegraph message broke off at this point, probably because the wires had burned up.

When another meteoric ball of flames crossed to the South Division, it struck the gasworks, where a large

In the early morning hours, Chicago mayor Roswell B. Mason set to work in the Cook County Courthouse, dispatching urgent requests for help by telegram to surrounding communities.

holding tank of volatile fuel erupted in the intense heat, adding to the explosive flames. The gas-fed streetlights throughout Chicago flickered and then went out. Yet the city remained aglow with the light of the immense blaze. Even the river, now slick with grease and oil, burned with flames.

By midnight a wall of fire was sweeping through the flimsy, closely built wooden structures of Conley's Patch. "Right and left the fire spread, travelling among the dry tenements, thickly distributed, at a rate of speed faster than a man could walk," the *Chicago Tribune* later reported. Grasping rosaries, crosses, and whatever possessions they could grab quickly—dolls, letters, dresses—the men, women, and children of Conley's Patch ran out into the streets, the air filled with their screams of terror. Most of the residents escaped, but some—most of them sick and elderly—were consumed by the quick-moving wall of fire, which measured more than 1,000 feet wide and 100 feet high.

Many of the Conley's Patch residents who had congregated in the West Division to watch the De Koven blaze stared helplessly from across the river as their homes went up in flames. Others desperately rushed toward the wooden bridges, trying to cross back to the South Division in an effort to save their families, pushing futilely against the rush of panicked people trying to flee the burning area.

The two separate fires from Conley's Patch and the gasworks soon combined to create an even greater inferno, blowing onward toward the heart of downtown Chicago, in the direction of the Cook County Courthouse. There, city officials were making every effort to deal with the blaze. Sixty-six-year-old Roswell B. Mason, the mayor of Chicago, had reached his administrative office in the courthouse at about midnight. Over the course of the next few hours, he received reports of the fire's progress, as well as information about the damage and destruction it was causing. As he tracked the fire's destructive path through the city, Mason dispatched several urgent telegrams, asking the nearby communities for assistance:

CHICAGO IS IN FLAMES. SEND YOUR
WHOLE DEPARTMENT TO HELP US.

The surrounding municipalities quickly rallied to help save Chicago. The cities of Milwaukee, Wisconsin; Cincinnati, Ohio; Bloomington, Illinois; and Pittsburgh,

Pennsylvania, were among those that dispatched their firefighters and equipment—ladder wagons, hoses, and steamers. Although Milwaukee had only four steam engines, it sent Chicago three steamers and their crews, leaving itself vulnerable that night to any potential fires.

Meanwhile, along the southern edge of the fire, in the South Division, James Hildreth, a former city alderman, was organizing an attempt to fight the fire by using explosives. He had procured about 2,500 pounds of charges that he decided to set off to create a firebreak. By leveling some wooden buildings that were in the direct

At approximately 2:20 Monday morning, the massive firestorm silenced the great bell of the courthouse, which fell in a blaze of burning embers that one onlooker described as "a snowstorm lit by colored fire."

line of the fire, Hildreth reasoned, there would be nothing flammable for the fire to burn. These firebreaks could stop the path of the ever growing fire.

But like the efforts of almost anyone else daring to fight the willful blaze, Hildreth's attempts proved unsuccessful. He did not have enough black powder to knock down the buildings that lay in the flames' path, and only succeeded in shattering a handful of windows and blowing down a wall. His actions, unfortunately, provided a pathway into the neighborhood, exposing it to the impending wrath of the fire, rather than protecting it. Even if Hildreth had been able to level the buildings, the ferocious winds would almost certainly have propelled the fire onward anyway.

Many more volunteers tried to stop the northward advance of the South Division blaze. Standing on the flammable tar-and-wood roofs of buildings, they attempted to beat out small fires that ignited wherever showering sparks landed. The sky was filled with flying cinders. It was as if Chicago had been hit by "an illuminated snowstorm," one resident later explained. The fire raced on, and it was heading straight for the Cook County Courthouse.

As the blaze loomed close, Mathias Schaffer and another watchman struggled desperately on the smoldering courthouse roof, trying to extinguish the small fires that flared up amid the falling sparks and firebrands. But just as soon as the men stomped out one small blaze, another would take its place. The heat grew more and more intense as the huge fire consumed nearby buildings. Then, suddenly, a large chunk of blazing wood crashed into the courthouse's wooden cupola, and an unstoppable, ravenous blaze erupted.

Mayor Mason immediately ordered that the courthouse be evacuated. Smoke rushed in through openings in the ceiling and the floor. Prisoners housed in the basement jail screamed in terror, fearful that they would be forgotten and left to burn alive. Mason acted quickly, ordering the release of most of the convicts, although the more dangerous criminals were taken away in chains to another location.

One eyewitness described the scene in front of the courthouse: "The Courthouse Park was filled with people, who appeared to be huddled together in a solid mass, helpless and astounded. The whole air was lit with falling cinders."

At 2:20 A.M. the courthouse tower collapsed, and its giant bell, which had tolled so many warnings of fire to the people of Chicago, plummeted through the ceiling to the ground below. Its resounding crash could be heard from as far as a mile away.

"Billows of fire were rolling over the business palaces of the city and swallowing up their contents," eyewitness Horace White recalled. Among the grand buildings to fall before the fire was the stately Crosby Opera House, located in the commercial district of the South Division.

"A Frightful Discord"

W hen *Tribune* editor Horace White first learned about the fire, he was not worried. From his home on Michigan Avenue, about four blocks from the newspaper office, he had heard the courthouse bell tolling the alarm, but as the bell rang so frequently he had ignored the warning. After a while, however, White noticed that the alarm tolls changed and now indicated a general alarm. In other words, the fire had grown from a small one to a much larger and more danger-ous blaze. When White looked out the window, he could see "a great light" in the sky to the southwest.

Still unconcerned, White decided that he might as well go to the *Tribune* newspaper office to write a story on the fire. But as soon as he

A driver fights skittish horses and furious flames in an attempt to take his wagonload of household goods to safety. Illustrator Alfred Waud captured that moment and many others from the Great Fire in sketches made using pencil, chalk, and white paint.

stepped outside his home, he grasped the seriousness of the situation. Not only was the fire dangerously close but it was also spreading rapidly.

White would later describe his first impressions of the blaze in a newspaper account published in the *Cincinnati Commercial:* "The fire was moving northward like ocean surf on a sand beach. It had already traveled an eighth of a mile and was far beyond control. A column of flame would shoot up from a burning building, catch the force of the wind, and strike the next one, which in turn would perform the same direful office for its neighbor. It was simply indescribable in its terrible grandeur."

Horace White hurried on to check the Tribune Building, which was just a few blocks away at Madison and Dearborn Streets. It was one of several fireproof structures in the downtown area, having been built of granite blocks, with iron beams and brick interior walls. Indeed, the Tribune Building had all of the makings of a fireproof structure—except for, unfortunately, its roof, which like so many Chicago roofs was made of tar-covered wood.

When White reached the office, he saw that *Tribune* workers were hosing down the building's highly flammable roof and stamping out any burning cinders that landed. From the Tribune Building, he could see the flames breaking out on the roof of the Cook County Courthouse, and he knew that the blaze would soon arrive in the business district. Yet when the great firestorm reached the area, White was relieved to see that the Tribune Building had indeed proved to be fireproof: "We saw the tall buildings on the opposite sides of the two streets melt down in a few minutes without scorching ours. The heat broke the plate-glass windows in the lower stories, but not the upper ones. After the fire in our neighborhood had spent its force, the editorial and composing rooms did not even smell of smoke."

Confident that his office building would survive the massive fire that was destroying much of the rest of Chicago, the *Tribune* editor returned home to see to the safety of his family. Well aware that the fire threatened his home, White helped his family hastily pack their belongings into a hired wagon. Then he and the driver headed out, determined to save the household's possessions by taking them to a friend's home for safekeeping. Having successfully accomplished that mission, White went back for his family.

The return trip proved more difficult. White had to pass through thick clouds of choking smoke and haze as the fire swept nearer. When he finally reached his family, White learned that the fire had indeed come close— his home had gone up in flames. But fortunately his family and the servants were safe. The Whites quickly climbed into their wagon and fled to safety, first to a friend's home on Wabash Avenue, but eventually further south of the blazing city.

*   *   *

From the Cook County Courthouse the flames had continued to toss firebrands before the driving wind, pushing the blaze eastward into the South Division's downtown business district, now a mile-wide firestorm of intense heat. There, even the most imposing iron and stone buildings could not withstand the high temperatures as the immense flames swept through. The mortar in brick buildings dissolved, marble crumbled, and iron melted. Within about five minutes the firestorm consumed some of Chicago's proudest buildings, including the unfinished Grand Pacific Hotel, the post office, the

custom house, Crosby's Opera House, and the Field and Lieter dry goods store.

When the part owner of the *Chicago Tribune*, 58-year-old William Bross, learned of the fire he left his house to check the *Tribune* newspaper offices. After satisfying himself that the Tribune Building was safe, Bross continued on to Washington and Franklin Streets, where he owned a hotel. There, he watched in horror as the fire enveloped the building in flames, then he tried to retreat back home. He later described the sight:

> At this time the fire was the most grandly magnificent scene that one can conceive. The Courthouse, Post Office, Farwell Hall, Tremont House, Sherman

A panic-stricken population fills Dearborn Street as the elegant Tremont House catches fire. Chicago resident William Bross described seeing "crowds of men, women, and children ... running first in one direction, then in another, shouting and crying in their terror."

House, and all the splendid buildings on La Salle and Wells streets were burning with a sublimity of effect. . . . Crowds of men, women, and children were huddling away, running first in one direction, then in another, shouting and crying in their terror, and trying to save anything they could lay their hands on, no matter how trivial in value; while every now and then explosions, which seemed almost to shake the solid earth, would reverberate through the air and add to the terrors of the poor people.

As the streets buzzed with terrified people, blazing buildings collapsed with thunderous crashes, the flying fragments of limestone shattering to the ground.

*   *   *

The fire roared on, still spreading mostly to the north and east as the relentless winds drove the flames forward. Frightened citizens crowded the roads, confused as to what to do and where to go. In hazy, smoke-filled streets men struggled with heavily laden carts and wagons that overflowed with clothing, furniture, and household goods. The *Chicago Tribune* would later paint a grim, yet realistic, picture of the crowds and the chaos as the ocean of flames in the South Division pushed eastward toward Lake Michigan, bearing down on the panic-stricken residents of Wabash Avenue:

Ladies dressed in elegant costumes, put on with a view of preserving them, and with costly apparel of all kinds thrown over their arms and shoulders, staggered along under the unwonted burden. Poor women with mattresses on their heads, or weighed down with furniture, tottered with weary steps up the crowded street. Nearly everyone wore a stern expression, and moved on without a word, as if they had braced up their minds

to endure the worst without manifesting any emo-
tion. . . . Poor little children shivered in the cold night
air and looked with wildly-open eyes upon the scenes
they could not comprehend. . . . Women would go by
with dogs in their arms—their pets being all they had
saved from the ruins of their homes.

The streets were littered with abandoned furniture,
priceless oil paintings, and trunks filled with expensive
clothing and other goods—some of which had been set
ablaze by showers of falling cinders. Crying children
wandered aimlessly, separated from parents in the noisy
press of the crowds. Wealthy women, weighed down by
masses of jewelry, hauled mattresses on their heads
alongside the poorer immigrant women. People struggled to save sick or invalid family members, carrying
them in makeshift chairs and litters.

South Division residents surged ahead, searching for
an escape from the conflagration that had engulfed their
neighborhoods. Carrying whatever they could salvage,
with the heat on their backs and hot air burning their
lungs, many refugees headed for the West or North
Divisions. The wooden bridges they had to cross became
jammed with panicked horses, overloaded wagons, and
frantic crowds.

Other refugees headed east, toward the beaches
along Lake Michigan, where they gathered at the Basin,
an area of the lakefront where the Illinois Central Railroad Company had built a breakwater. This protective
wall, which normally would shield a beach from strong
waves, now provided an obstruction to the raging fire.
Dazed Chicago citizens would stay the night at the
Basin, sitting on furniture and trunks that they had managed to salvage from their homes. As the Great Fire
grew closer and its swirling sparks and embers

threatened, the frightened citizens of Chicago waded out into the icy lake waters as far as possible, trying to keep safe from the roaring flames.

*   *   *

New York assemblyman Alexander Frear was visiting his brother's family in Chicago that fateful October evening. In an article later published in the *New York World* he described his experiences trying to help his sister-in-law and his two young nieces and nephew. (His brother was out of town that night.) Frear's adventures during that time took him back and forth between the burning fires in several neighborhoods of Chicago's West and South Divisions.

Like everyone else in the city that night, Frear did not realize the severity of the fire at first. He saw the first orange glow in the West Division as early as 10:00 P.M., as he was leaving the Sherman House hotel, in the South Division. He did not think anything of it, however, despite the fact that his brother's home was in that area. Like many other people in Chicago that warm fall evening, he thought it might be interesting to take a look at the fire and watch its progress.

As Frear headed towards his brother's home near Des Plaines Street, he noticed the mood of the people around him changing from interest to alarm and panic. They were beginning to realize that this fire was unlike the previous blazes that had befallen Chicago. It was huge, out of control, and spreading quickly. There seemed no guaranteed safe place to escape from it.

Now Frear hastened to reach his sister-in-law's home, but the journey became increasingly difficult. "[T]he walks were so crowded with people and the cinders were blown so thickly and fast that I found it was impossible. . . . it was difficult to see anything on account of the cinders," he recalled later. Once Frear reached his brother's home, he gathered together the three frightened children and in a hired coach escorted them to safety in a South Division neighborhood about a mile away, near Wabash Avenue.

But soon after returning to fetch the children's mother, Frear learned that the flames had reached the neighborhood that he had just left. In a panic, he and his sister-in-law tried to hurry back to the children, but their progress was slowed by the fire's chaos. "The roadway was full of people, and the din of voices and the melee of horses rendered unmanageable by the falling embers was terrible," he noted. When he and Mrs. Frear finally reached the Wabash block, they found it ablaze.

Fortunately, despite the confusion, Frear encountered a friend who informed him that the children had been moved to safety and were now at the nearby St. James Hotel. But when Frear and his sister-in-law arrived there, the children were not to be found. Thinking he might have misunderstood the name of the hotel where the children had been taken, Frear headed out on his own to check for them at the Sherman House. But instead of finding the children there, he found the fire. Workers had managed to put out the blazes that had sprung up on the hotel's rooftop, but the building was in an uproar, with the hallways shrouded in dense black smoke and guests stumbling about in a state of terror and confusion.

John R. Chapman, an artist for *Harper's Weekly*, was also staying at the Sherman House that night. After escaping from the smoldering hotel into the streets, he eventually made his way to the Randolph Street Bridge, where he sketched the chaotic scene. Later published in *Harper's*, the striking image would eventually by copied

Outside the Sherman House, frightened mobs struggled on foot, carrying belongings, children, and invalids, while Chicago's wealthier residents attempted to flee by horse and carriage. In the crush and confusion of the crowds, family members often lost sight of one another.

by several other artists and engravers for other periodicals as well.

Chapman later described the scene he had illustrated: "For nearly two miles to the right of me the flames and smoke were rising from the ruins and ashes of dwellings, warehouses, lumberyards, the immense gas-works." To the left, he explained, was a grain elevator that had been turned into "a living coal . . . sending upward a sheet of flame and smoke a thousand feet high."

But the sounds of the chaotic scene made an even stronger impression on the artist. The wind, he said, was "moaning," and the raging flames were roaring, mixed in with screams from the crowd and the "shrill whistling of the tugs," as tugboats on the river below tried to push lumber ships out of harm's way. Chapman later wrote that the "frightful discord of sounds will live in memory while life shall last."

As firefighters battled the blaze, they attempted to communicate amid the commotion by shouting to one another through voice trumpets, which amplified their voices. A *Chicago Post* article, published on October 17, would echo Chapman's observations in a one-sentence description that captures the incredible scene and sounds at the height of the fire: "Everywhere dust, smoke, flame, heat, thunder of falling walls, crackle of fire, hissing of water, panting of engines, shouts, braying of trumpets, wind, tumult, and uproar."

*　　　　*　　　　*

Panicked for the safety of his brother's children, Frear continued his search with the help of his 18-year-old nephew, whom he encountered in the St. James Hotel. Together they headed off in a wagon toward Wabash Avenue and into the cinder and smoke-filled streets of the city. "We drove as rapidly as we could . . . the wind sweeping the embers after us in furious waves. . . . The storm of falling fire seemed to increase every second, and it was as much as we could do to protect ourselves from the burning rain and guide the horse through the flying people and hurrying vehicles."

The scene on Wabash Avenue was of absolute terror, Frear noted.

> All the mansions were being emptied with the greatest disorder and the greatest excitement. Nobody endeavored [to stop] the flames now. A mob of men and women, all screaming and shouting, ran about wildly, crossing each other's paths, and intercepting each other

as if deranged. We tried to force our way along the avenue, which was already littered with costly furniture, some of it burning in the street under falling sparks, but it was next to impossible.

Sometime around two or three o'clock Monday morning, Frear acknowledged the futility of trying to find three young children in the midst of the fire's smoky chaos and confusion. He and his nephew returned to the St. James Hotel, where rumors were spreading as quickly as the fire everyone sought to escape. The bridges were burning, someone claimed, and all escape routes to the north and west would soon be cut off. As frantic guests tried to cram their way out of the door and into the streets, Frear became separated from his nephew.

Near exhaustion, Frear thought of yet another refuge where the children might be. He quickly set off for the Tremont House, where he fruitlessly searched several lower floors of the hotel despite the fiery blaze enveloping its upper stories. In despair, he returned to neighborhoods already explored, including Wabash Avenue, which was in chaos:

> I went through to Wabash Avenue and here the thoroughfare was utterly choked with all manner of goods and people. Everybody who had been forced from the other end of the town by the advancing flames had brought some article with him, and, as further progress was delayed, if not completely stopped by the river— the bridges of which were also choked—most of them, in their panic, abandoned their burdens, so that the streets and sidewalks presented the most astonishing wreck. Valuable oil paintings, books, pet animals, musical instruments, toys, mirrors, and bedding, were trampled under foot.

Fortunately, the rumors about burned bridges to the north and west proved false. Although Frear couldn't find his nephew, he did manage to find a bridge that would take him back to his sister-in-law's house, in the West Division. Although heavily damaged, the wooden bridge was sturdy enough to cross. Just minutes after safely reaching the other side, however, Frear watched the structure catch fire, setting the boats beneath it ablaze as its burning pieces dropped into the river below.

An engraving of Randolph Street Bridge, based on a drawing by John R. Chapman. As he sketched the chaotic scene, Chapman was struck by the "frightful discord of sounds" around him as the wind howled, the flames roared, and the tightly packed crowds on the bridge screamed in panic.

"The Cry Was 'North! North!'"

Soon after the courthouse tower tumbled to the ground at 2:30 that morning, the wind propelled a chunk of blazing wood across the northern branch of the Chicago River and into the North Division of the city. The firebrand landed in a railroad car filled with kerosene and combusted on impact into a wild torrent of flames. In just seconds the blazing inferno had established itself in the North Division.

Around two in the morning earth-shattering explosions emanating from the middle of the city had awakened two sisters residing in Chicago's North Division. Soon after, a neighbor frantically knocked at their door, urging them to quickly gather their most valuable possessions and evacuate. The flames were rapidly advancing in the direction of their neighborhood.

But there was not enough time. Within seconds a wall of flaming cinders crashed into their door. Miraculously the two sisters managed to escape. As they evacuated toward the north, one carried a parrot in its cage, and the other dragged a trunk. When they looked back at their home, all they could see was a "wall of fire . . . steadily advancing on our midnight helplessness."

Although the firefighters tried their best to battle the destructive blaze, they too were at its mercy. The men from Engine Company No. 14 became trapped in a narrow alley when, in an instant, a gust of flames encircled their vehicle. Although the firefighters were able to make their way through the fiery walls to safety, they had to abandon the precious engine to the flames. Showing remarkable courage and presence of mind, the firemen continued to fight on, despite the harrowing incident that they had just survived.

As the Great Fire progressed through the North Division, it soon reached the city waterworks, located near Pine Street and Chicago Avenue. Although the Gothic-style structure was built of fire-resistant solid limestone, it was also covered by a flimsy—and quite flammable—wooden roof. That fatal flaw proved catastrophic when a piece of burning timber catapulted onto the top of the waterworks building at around 3 A.M., and angry flames quickly engulfed the building. The roof collapsed onto the pumping station, and its four powerful pumping engines came to a halt. Chicago's water supply was cut off.

The flames did not affect the nearby water tower, which suffered only minor damage. The tower still held some water, which continued to flow for a while from a few city reservoirs. But without the station pumps, there was essentially no more water for the burning city of Chicago.

The waves of flame pressed relentlessly on, next setting ablaze the State Street Bridge. Stables, warehouses,
and breweries there promptly caught fire, followed soon
afterward by the luxurious mansions in the residential
areas near Cass, Huron, Ontario, and Dearborn Streets.
Once it had destroyed the water pumping station, nothing could be done to slow the fire's progress. In less than
an hour the blaze hungrily consumed 11 blocks—
roughly a square mile—in Chicago's North Division,
destroying this neighborhood faster than any other in
the city.

With no water, firemen could fight only the blazes
burning near the Chicago River, which provided the
steam engines with the water to pump. And without
water to hose down their wooden roofs, fireproof structures such as the South Division's Tribune Building were
no longer impervious to the flames. Soon it and many
other grand "fireproof" structures like it fell victim to
ravenous flames. Even with the support of additional fire
companies, which were arriving from neighboring cities,
Chicago's fire department could do little more to stop the
conflagration from continuing its deadly march to the
north. There was simply no water to fight the flames.

The fire continued to overwhelm the North Division. As the sky glowed a fluorescent yellow-orange in
the dead of night, people clad only in their nightshirts
and nightgowns ran up and down the streets in terror. In
the midst of the panic some became separated from their
families; others screamed and moaned in terror and confusion as they realized they were in danger of becoming
entrapped in an ever tightening circle of flames.

Some refugees fled to the Sands, an area along Lake
Michigan just north of the Chicago River. Those not
trapped at the Sands traveled further north to the un-
developed, open areas of prairie outside Chicago. In his

Groups of refugees, their journey captured on paper by artist Alfred Waud, head for safety in the open prairie lands to the north of Chicago, beyond the city limits at Fullerton Avenue.

account of the fire A. S. Clapp described the feelings of the refugees:

> Without thinking, [they were] possessed by one thought—on, onward—away from the burning city to the green country beyond. Nobody might stop to rest; he was pressed on by others as tired as himself. Men pulled buggies loaded with all they had on earth; women carried burdens larger than themselves; children pushed baby carriages containing the little saved from their homes. On they went to Fullerton avenue to scatter over the prairie—to drop in their tracks and wait for they knew not what.

City resident Aurelia R. King, the wife of a merchant, evacuated with her children at her skirts. "The cry was 'North! North!'" she explained later. "You could not conceive anything more fearful. The wind was like a tornado, and I held fast to my little ones, fearing they would be lifted from my sight. I could only think of Sodom or Pompeii, and truly I thought the day of judgement had come."

King and her children fled to the safety of Lincoln Park, a 230-acre area located next to a cemetery and along the banks of Lake Michigan. When the fugitives arrived, they joined thousands of other refugees, whose numbers eventually would reach 30,000.

Side by side stood the masses of people huddled together, no longer bound by the powerful social and economic boundaries that normally kept them separate from one another. Law-abiding citizens and criminals alike fled the flames, all sharing the same fear and desire to save their lives. The rich stood alongside the poor. One historical account describes the erasure of social barriers: "Mr. McCormick, the millionaire of the reaper trade, and other north-side nabobs [kept company] with the humblest laborer, the lowest vagabond, and the meanest harlot. Once they settled themselves, there was little they could do but bear witness to this calamity beyond comprehension."

As the hours wore on, the refugees dealt with the situation as best they could. Most of the displaced citizens huddled at the water's edge, where they remained surprisingly calm. Many agreed that the end of the world seemed at hand, apparently agreeing with the religious zealots who in the midst of the chaos had stood on street corners proclaiming the fire as God's judgment on the world. Some refugees prayed throughout the night; others passed the time singing songs as the hours dragged on.

By noon on Monday fires in the North Division had reached North Avenue and the southern edges of Lincoln Park. One eyewitness described how the blaze reached the edges of their temporary sanctuary, destroying the nearby cemetery: "The flames . . . made havoc among the dead, burning down the wooden monuments, and shattering stone vaults to fragments."

While most Chicagoans were fleeing the terrible fire, some took the opportunity to engage in crime, arson, and profiteering. Although these unfortunate incidents did occur, accounts published later by the newspapers tended to sensationalize the extent of the crimes.

Newspapers later reported that looters stole whatever they could gather from the doomed stores and businesses. Tabloids printed accounts of deliberate arson, such as the story of how one young boy nonchalantly ignited a clothesline saturated with kerosene and tossed it into a building on Thirty-second Street. The *Chicago Tribune* reported that many drivers of wagons and carts charged exorbitant prices to haul away families' goods. The article accused these men of "turning up their noses at offers of amounts less than they demanded. This class of people made great profit out of the calamities of their fellow citizens. Their pockets may be heavy today, but their consciences, if they have any, should still be heavier."

Yet Horace White would later write of many kindly acts he saw as he and his family fled the city: "The poor helped the rich, and the rich helped the poor (if anybody could be called rich at such a time) to get on with their loads."

By sunrise on Monday morning, much of Chicago lay devastated—transformed from a once bustling, vibrant city to a mess of burning, flattened streets. As one North Division resident, Del Moore, surveyed the area that morning, she had a premonition that although the situation didn't seem like it could get much worse, something horrible was about to happen. It was then she heard someone cry out, "The lumberyard is on fire!" Nearby stacks of timber lit up like kindling to a bonfire and were soon completely consumed by the powerful flames.

That Monday morning, even as the fire still blazed, several city leaders had begun to organize to address relief efforts for the devastated city. They realized that Chicago needed help not only with stopping the fire but also with providing food, shelter, and medical attention for its many displaced residents. Government officials were concerned with maintaining law and order as well.

Since the Chicago city government's offices had been destroyed when the Cook County Courthouse fell, a new meeting place was established—the First Congregational Church, located at the corner of West Washington and Ann Streets. The building was in an area of the West Division considered safe from the fire.

The Chicago Common Council president, Charles C. P. Holden, invited several elected officials and prominent citizens to the emergency meeting, which Mayor Mason

Approximately 30,000 North Division residents sought refuge in Lincoln Park, which they reached by passing through a cemetery. Many exhausted refugees camped out among the dead, trapped between the crowds, the graveyard to the south, and Lake Michigan to the east.

joined later in the afternoon. By 3 P.M. he had signed a proclamation to be posted throughout the city that included the following assurances and directives:

WHEREAS, In the Providence of God, to whose will we humbly submit, a terrible calamity has befallen our city which demands of us our best efforts for the preservation of order and relief of suffering, be it known that the faith and credit of the City of Chicago is hereby pledged for the necessary expenses for the relief of the suffering.

Public order will be preserved. The police and special police now being appointed will be responsible for the maintenance of the peace and protection of property.

All officers and men of the Fire Department and Health Department will act as special policemen without further notice.

The Mayor and Comptroller will give vouchers for all supplies furnished by the different relief committees.

The headquarters of the City Government will be at the Congregational Church, corner of West Washington and Ann Streets.

All persons are warned against any act tending to endanger property. Persons caught in any depredation will be immediately arrested.

With the help of God, order and peace and private property will be preserved.

The City Government and the committee of citizens pledge themselves to the community to protect them, and prepare the way for a restoration of public and private welfare.

It is believed the fire has spent its force, and all will soon be well.

The mayor's proclamation promised that city credit would pay for relief efforts, the government would establish a force that would help preserve public order, and that anyone caught looting would be arrested. The order also informed Chicago citizens that the First Congregational Church was serving, at least temporarily, as the site of the city government.

The proclamation also referred to the establishment of a relief committee, established by the authority of the mayor and the common council. This relief committee was made up of citizens and elected officials from the North, South, and West Divisions. The council decided that the committee would be responsible for the distribution of any food, supplies, and money that the city received.

In an effort to keep prices fair and affordable for the many needy residents of Chicago, the council set a fixed price for bread at eight cents per 12-ounce loaf. The group also had the foresight to enact several other important temporary rules, including a ban on smoking, a limit on saloon operating hours, and a decree forbidding wagon drivers from charging more than their normal rates. The council also determined that public buildings would be kept open as shelters for the homeless. Soon after the Monday meeting ended, Mayor Mason sent out pleas to various cities by telegraph for emergency relief.

*   *   *

After making his way to what he thought would be the site of his sister-in-law's burned-out home in the West Division, Alexander Frear was shocked to find the house still standing and his missing 18-year-old nephew inside. With relief, Frear learned that his sister-in-law was safe as well, staying with friends on Huron Street, although she remained frantically worried about her missing children. Overcome with anxiety and

Finally, as the rains fell late Monday night, the Great Fire came to an end. However, areas such as these riverside coal heaps continued to smolder and burn for several more weeks.

exhaustion, Frear collapsed on the floor. He later explained, "I was wet and scorched and bedraggled. My clothes were burnt and full of holes on my arms and shoulders and back. . . . I fell down in the hallway and went to sleep."

His rest lasted a mere 30 minutes, after which he was suddenly roused with the news that the fire again threatened his sister-in-law's safety and that he needed to help move her to another refuge. Several more hours would pass before Frear received word that the children were alive and safe, having been moved by friends to the Riverside section of Chicago. Only then could the emotionally and physically drained man climb into bed and escape into the deep sleep of a well-deserved rest.

*   *   *

The Great Chicago Fire continued to burn throughout Monday, following its relentless path as far north as the city limits at Fullerton Avenue. At 5 P.M. the Chicago Avenue Bridge fell to the flames, cutting off a significant escape route to the west.

Finally, at around 11:00 that night, a cool drizzle began to fall, the droplets of rain mixing in with the hissing embers and smoky haze. At the sight of rain Chicago's weary refugees began shouting and dancing with joy and disbelief. A few hours later the drizzle became a steady downpour. By three o'clock on Tuesday morning, rain was washing over the smoldering city, sending up clouds of steam and smoke. One woman expressed the relief felt by thousands of Chicago residents: "I never felt so grateful in my life as to hear the rain pour down at three o'clock this morning. That stopped the fire."

But the Great Fire did not entirely stop with the rain. In certain areas small pockets of flames burned for several more days, especially fires fed by heaps of coal or other fuels. But the downpour certainly prevented the flames from spreading any further, and the deluge made the smaller blazes easier to extinguish.

By the time it ended, the Great Chicago Fire had raged more than 27 hours, leaving a vast swath of destruction in its wake. At least 100,000 people were homeless. Although the fire was over, Chicago's recovery from the devastation was just beginning.

Chicago
in Ruins

The one small wooden shed under construction just after the Great Fire contrasts starkly with the devastation surrounding it. The intense heat of the blaze razed the brick and stone structures of Chicago and reduced its wooden buildings to ashes.

The *Chicago Evening Journal*, in its one-page edition published on Monday, October 9, captured the emotions of the city's residents: "The scene of ruin and devastation is beyond the power of words to describe. Never, in the history of the world, has such a scene of extended, terrible and complete destruction, by conflagration, been recorded; and never has a more frightful scene of panic, distress and horror been witness among a helpless, sorrowing, suffering population."

Little remained of the original Chicago after the October 8–9 fire. The 2,000 acres devastated by the fire, which covered an area about four miles long and an average of three-quarters of a mile wide, came to be known as the Burnt District. The Great Chicago Fire destroyed 17,500 buildings,

A view of the Burnt
District, which covered
more than 2,000 acres.
The white areas indicate
the locations of many
prominent buildings lost
to the fire, including the
gasworks (at Adams and
Market) and the Cook
County Courthouse (at
Clark and Washington).

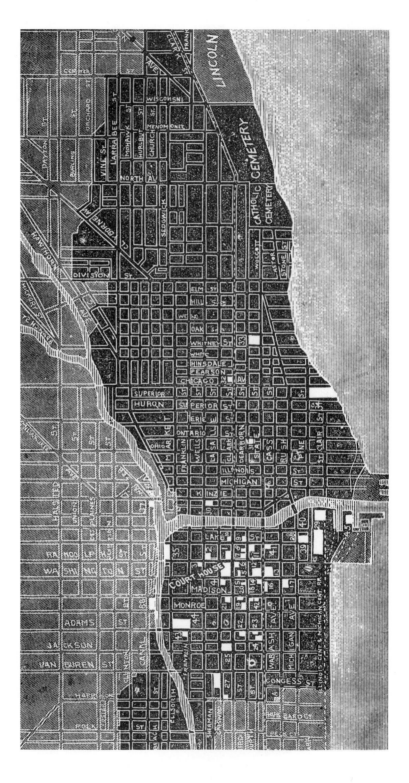

73 miles of streets, and 120 miles of sidewalks, not to mention numerous trees, shrubs, and flowering plants.

Joseph Medill, the 48-year-old co-owner of the *Chicago Tribune*, described the scenes of devastation:

> The proud and stately city of yesterday . . . had sunk into cellars and basements. What had hours before been the mart of commerce was now an indescribable chaos of broken columns, fallen walls, streets covered with debris, melted metal, charred and blackened trees standing like spectres. Thousands of columns of smoke and enveloping tongues of flame still rose out of the tumbling ruins. . . . Great [grain] elevators had disappeared. The tall spires of churches, the Courthouse dome, the stately blocks that were the pride of the city and the admiration of visitors, the noted landmarks . . . everything had disappeared.

One North Division resident, Stephen L. Robinson, whose home had come through the blaze intact, later explored his neighborhood in search of other buildings that had survived. He found that only a few homes still stood, including real estate millionaire Mahlon Ogden's mansion on Lafayette Street and the house of police officer Richard Bellinger. The North Division had been hit the hardest by the fire: approximately 13,300 of 13,800 buildings in that section of the city were destroyed. Although fewer lives were lost there than in the South Division, almost 75,000 residents of the North Division were left homeless.

In fact, very few homes remained standing throughout much of the Burnt District. In the South Division, an area known as the Lind Block survived. And in the West Division, the cottage of the O'Learys, in whose barn the immense conflagration first began, stood intact amid a surrounding sea of ashes.

The *Evening Journal* summed up the losses in terms of commercial damage to the city: "All the principal hotels, all the public buildings, all the banks, all the newspaper offices, all the places of amusement, nearly all the great business edifices, nearly all the railroad depots, the water works, the gas works, several churches, and thousand of private residences and stores have been consumed. The proud, noble magnificent Chicago of yesterday is to-day a mere shadow of what it was."

But for most people the immediate concern was not any commercial loss; the top priority was finding missing loved ones—children, husbands, wives, and friends—who had become separated from one another in the smoke and confusion of the fire. Frantic families checked churches and other relief areas, as well as Lincoln Park, the gathering area of many refugees. With no place left to go after the fire, many had simply remained there, living in tents and other makeshift housing. Another alternative was to keep vigil at the site of one's burned-out residence in hopes that the loved ones would eventually appear.

The last place people wanted to look was the morgue. A temporary morgue was established in a stable where the charred corpses were laid out in rows. Only four or five people at a time were allowed to view and help identify the bodies, which were usually burned beyond recognition.

Frank Luzerne later wrote about the Chicago fire in his book *The Lost City!* He remembered with horror the sight of the disfigured bodies, and described with graphic detail the condition of one corpse recovered from the debris: "The hair was completely burned off his head and body; the features were blackened and distorted with pain; the swollen lips were wide apart, disclosing the glistening teeth, and imparting a horrid grin, such only as agonizing death can stamp upon the face. The flesh was bloated to an astonishing size. The poor wretch was roasted alive."

Eventually, officials estimated that close to 300 people died in the fire, although only 120 bodies were dug out of the rubble. Some of the missing might have fallen in the river or drowned in the lake. Others may have died in the fire, where the intense heat cremated their bodies.

Many homeless left Chicago immediately after the fire, but those who remained had to camp out in city parks and open areas. Some of these survivors demonstrated remarkable resiliency and creativity in establishing shelters for themselves. One Chicago resident described how a homeless woman set up a comfortable environment for her sick husband. The wife had scavenged a piano packing case, set it on its side so that the lid blocked the wind, and arranged a makeshift bed inside for her husband to rest comfortably. She even hooked a candle to the top of the case, which provided her with ample light to read to him.

In the days following the fire, stories of arson, looting, and violence circulated, lent credence by newspapers, which published many unconfirmed tales. "The city is infested with a horde of thieves, burglars, and cutthroats, bent on plunder, and who will not hesitate to burn, pillage, and even murder, as opportunity may seem to offer to them to do so with safety," the *Chicago Evening Journal* reported a day after the fire. Cassius Milton Wicker, a Chicago and Northwestern Railroad freight agent told his family in Vermont, "With the close of the fire, or rather conflagration, our troubles have not closed. Roughs and thieves from all parts of the country flocked here for plunder."

It is likely such extreme statements were based more on fears than on facts. With the large-scale destruction of

Troops patrolled what seemed like a battle-ravaged city, which by martial law was under the command of Lt. Gen. Philip H. Sheridan. In this illustration, a soldier questions two passersby.

a way of life, city residents were struggling to make sense out of the disaster and were fearful of the actions of others. To ease these concerns and assure Chicagoans that the city government would protect its residents, Mayor Mason declared martial law, under the direction of Lt. Gen. Philip H. Sheridan. A renowned Civil War hero, the general lived in Chicago, where he commanded the Division of the Missouri from his office in the city's South Division.

Sheridan enlisted the help of regular troops, militia units, police, and a specially organized First Regiment of Chicago Volunteers. They enforced curfews, patrolled the streets, and guarded warehouses to discourage looting—sometimes with too much zeal, according to some critics.

As early as Monday evening, as the fire still burned, relief supplies began arriving in the devastated city as a sympathetic nation responded to Mayor Mason's telegraphed appeals for help. Trains from cities all over the United States delivered much-needed blankets, bedding, clothing, food, and cash contributions.

The mayor's proclamation had placed responsibility for relief efforts with the city government, which had quickly established emergency relief centers and enlisted Sheridan's troops to help distribute tents, food, and other supplies to the homeless. However, four days later, on October 13, Mason relinquished this job to the Chicago Relief and Aid Society (an organization founded in 1850 for the purpose of feeding and sheltering the poor). This group would oversee the distribution of supplies and monetary contributions that would eventually total about $5 million.

People across the country and around the world raised money and sent supplies for the Chicago relief effort. President Ulysses S. Grant sent $1,000 of his own money; the U.S. Army quartermaster stores sent 10,000 blankets. New York City sent nearly $1 million, Boston sent $400,000, and Philadelphia more than $300,000. Besides sending a donation of $435,000, England also included 12,000 books to replace those lost when Chicago libraries were destroyed.

The top priority of the relief effort was supplying needy city residents with food, shelter, and water. The Chicago Relief and Aid Society set about distributing the food donations and supplies of water at established relief areas.

Water was in short supply because of the loss of the waterworks pumping station, but entrepreneurs soon established businesses selling the precious liquid from

Sympathetic citizens in New York City, as well as in cities across the nation, raised funds and donated goods to help the homeless of Chicago. Once received, the contributions of food, clothing, and medical supplies were distributed by volunteers and members of the Chicago Relief and Aid Society.

water carts. Most city residents had to help themselves to the ready supply of water from nearby Lake Michigan, the Chicago River, or artesian wells located at the western end of the city. It would take eight days before city engineers managed to repair the water pumps and Chicago residents once again enjoyed running water. And then, because the water had stood in the pipes for so long, it was stagnant. For the next two weeks the contaminated water made thousands of people ill, especially children and the elderly.

The Burnt District remained hot for several days after the fire, preventing most people from surveying the damage to their homes and businesses. Some newspapers carried accounts of anxious businessmen opening red-hot safes among the ruins of their offices. Because the safes were still sizzling hot, so were their contents. Upon exposure to the air, papers and currency that had survived the conflagration immediately burst into flames.

Seven-year-old A. S. Chapman had accompanied his businessman father to his office just after the Great Fire. Years later he recalled the scene: "Along Randolph street safes have been dragged into the street. Men grimed with soot and ashes work like fiends with sledge hammers and steel wedges. It must have been practice to keep money in safes. Money—money; everybody looking for money in safes. I see men and women standing round a safe as its door is forced open. The air rushes in and I see their hopes turned to ashes as rolls of bills crumble at its touch."

Within a few days after the fire, virtually all of the burned buildings were leveled—about $200 million dollars in property, which was roughly one third of the estimated value of the entire city. About half of these buildings were insured, but many insurance companies did not make payments to the owners. The firms had declared bankruptcy because of the disaster.

After the fire, *Chicago Times* owner Wilbur Storey mourned, "The *Times* is dead. Chicago is gone, and I'm all through." Other newspaper owners responded much more quickly to the disaster. *Chicago Evening Journal* editor Andrew Shuman and *Tribune* co-owner Joseph Medill found a printer in the West Division. The *Evening Journal* managed to produce two issues on Monday, October 9; the *Tribune* published its first post-fire issue on Wednesday. Once Storey saw their success, he shook off his despair and concentrated on rebuilding the *Times*, which printed its first postfire issue on October 18.

News of the Great Fire had traveled quickly, and curiosity seekers soon flocked to the city. Tourists sought lodging with Chicago hotelmen and innkeepers, who were already scrambling to accommodate homeless residents.

Cameras were rare in 1871, and few people probably owned them in Chicago at the time of the fire. No photographs of the fire itself exist, perhaps because it traveled so fast and happened so quickly. Most pictures of the event itself are illustrations and sketches. Some were made during the fire by artist John Chapman, who had been in Chicago when the fire broke out. Another illustrator, Alfred R. Waud, was in St. Louis when he heard the news but quickly took a train to the burning city. Many illustrators, reporters, and photographers arrived after the Great Fire, eager to document the historic event. Three days after the blaze the *New York Tribune* reported, "The artists of the illustrated papers are seated at every [advantageous position], sketching for dear life against the closing of the mail."

All around the nation and the world people took a genuine interest in the Chicago fire. Many people learned of the disaster as it was occurring—informed as soon as the story reached their newspaper offices by telegraph. Readers followed the events of the fire for several reasons, the first being the horrible scale and complexity of it. The fire almost seemed too large to be believed. And the fact that the fire hit Chicago—a growing, bustling city—made the story even more captivating.

Unfortunately, the stories that some of the reporters told included healthy doses of exaggeration, supposition, and even outright lies. Newspaper articles often featured tales of heroic bravery, drunken brawls, and looters and thieves. Some stories ranged from sentimental accounts of the fire as a "test" of the spirit of Chicago, to critical, condemning analyses of why the fire occurred and of how it might have been prevented. The more spectacular the story, of course, the more newspapers were sold.

Over the previous years Chicago had endured its share of major blazes, but none had even come close to causing the devastating losses that resulted because of the Great Fire of 1871. The fire caused more than just widespread physical damage; it also inflicted painful psychological damage on the people of the city, whose lives—unlike the buildings—could not be as easily rebuilt.

The fire left 100,000 of Chicago's citizens homeless. Yet people did not lose just their houses but also the sources of their memories and sense of stability. Within a matter of a few days, their lives had moved from order to chaos, from prosperity to poverty, from hope to despair. By and large, they felt no sense of control over their destiny.

A week after the fire William H. Carter, president of Chicago's Board of Public Works, expressed these feelings in a letter written to his brother. Besides serving as an important firsthand account of the blaze, Carter's missive reveals his extreme emotional distress and sense of loss:

> I snatch the first moment I have had since one week ago tonight. Our beautiful city is in ruins. The greatest calamity that ever befell a city is upon us. . . .
>
> The Homestead built by my own hands out of my own hard earnings, is gone—a total wreck. . . . It was the first home I could call my own, where my children were born, where I had hoped to live to educate them, where I had welcomed kind brothers and sisters and

Many fugitives had escaped from the flames dressed only in the clothes they slept in, protected by the blankets they carried. In the days following the fire, the city government worked to provide these refugees with shelter and food. But fire survivors had much more to come to terms with: the despair of having lost their way of life.

friends in the past and where I had hoped to do it often in the future. . . .

Chicago is burned down but not despairing—she has the energy and push and will rise phoenix like from the ashes.

Carter's letter also demonstrates a remarkable sense of optimism and energy that seemed typical of Chicago's citizens, even in the face of such hardship. He compares Chicago to the ancient myth of the phoenix, a legendary bird that after being burned on a funeral pyre, emerges from the fire reborn. Many others would make the same analogy in the coming years as the residents of Chicago demonstrated their resilience.

Still, Mayor Mason realized that his citizens needed time to grieve and to meditate on the dramatic event they had just experienced. So he declared that Sunday, October 29, be set aside "as a special day of humiliation and prayer of humiliation for those past offenses against Almighty God, to which these severe afflictions were doubtless intended to lead our minds; of prayer for the relief and comfort of the suffering thousands in our midst; for the restoration of our material prosperity, especially for our lasting improvement as a people in reverence and obedience to God." Only after this solemn day of reflection did the Great Rebuilding begin.

Rebuilding on Dearborn Street. Among the impressive architectural structures of Dearborn Street lost to the fire were the Tribune Building, the Post Office and Custom House, and Crosby's Opera House.

Like a Phoenix from the Ashes

6

T he Chicago Relief and Aid Society set about establishing ways to help Chicago residents recover from the massive disaster. The organization divided the city into districts and opened offices and supply depots in each section.

For those Chicago residents ready to begin rebuilding their homes, the society distributed lumber to construct single-room structures, or "shelter houses." If the recipient did not own his or her own land, the family rented a plot on Michigan Avenue upon which to build. People dug among the rubble as well, scavenging bricks and hardware that could be salvaged for use in rebuilding. Workers filled carts with the fire's debris, which was dumped into Lake Michigan, south of the river, to create new land to build on.

One of the first retail businesses to open in downtown Chicago after the Great Fire, Schock, Bigford & Company sold wares such as apples, grapes, cigars, and tobacco.

Many makeshift businesses appeared among the ruins as well, established in newly erected sheds or stands. Other merchants placed broadsides, or posters, at the sites of their burned-out businesses, directing customers to their new locations. By the end of the first week after the fire, about 6,000 temporary residential and business structures had been erected; and construction on more than 200 permanent buildings had already begun.

Real estate agent William Kerfoot exemplified the spirit of the resilient Chicago community. He set up shop in a shack, ready for business just days after the fire. On the dilapidated building hung a testament to his willingness to persevere: "All gone but wife, children, and energy."

Two weeks after the fire, author Alfred Sewell strolled through the ruined city and commented on the contrast between Michigan Avenue before and after the fire. "Builders were busily engaged in constructing scores of one-story sheds for the temporary accommodation of merchants," he said, "and what was a fortnight ago one of the finest residence avenues in the world is now lined with board shanties."

Many Chicagoans were worried that businesses would leave the city after the Great Fire and relocate in nearby cities such as St. Louis and Milwaukee. One New Orleans paper predicted that Chicago would never recover: "Its prestige has passed away . . . its glory will be of the past, not the present." Business owners quickly responded to such threats to the city's public image, quickly pointing out the many Chicago industries and businesses that the fire had not reached. The city still had grain elevators, rail and shipping depots, and stockyards located west and south of the Burnt District. Scores of companies were setting up makeshift offices as well.

The city was certainly in a hurry to rebuild as quickly as possible, and this need created a demand for skilled laborers such as carpenters and bricklayers. Workers came from as far as 150 miles away to take these high-paying jobs, and at first, salaries soared. Unskilled laborers could earn as much as $2 a day; carpenters and bricklayers could earn up to $10 a day.

But with the influx of job seekers came a housing shortage. In response the landlords raised their rents, while employers kept workers' wages at the same levels. Carpenters and bricklayers organized strikes in an attempt to protest the situation but had little success. For the most part, the public condemned such actions as counter to the good of the city.

The Chicago Relief and Aid Society would operate until April 1874, overseeing the distribution of the $5 million in aid money that the city eventually received. The society's work covered six areas: contributions, distribution, employment, health, shelter, and transportation—each overseen by a separate committee.

The society met the needs of Chicago's homeless in many ways: It found jobs for more than 20,000 workers and provided medical care for 90,000 people, including vaccinations against smallpox for 64,000. The organization helped provide tools and appliances to those who needed them, issued free railroad passes to fire refugees, and worked to provide services that would expedite the rebuilding of Chicago. For example, in order to attract

Children play in the snow in front of the Washington Square Park barracks, constructed by the Relief and Aid Society to house the homeless poor. This development was built across the street from the manor of real estate millionaire Mahlon Ogden, whose home was the only mansion in the North Division to survive the fire.

construction workers, it designated that the shelter houses be reserved for skilled workers. For the homeless poor, the Chicago Relief and Aid Society eventually built four sets of barracks, which provided two furnished rooms each to 1,000 families.

However, a clear class distinction appeared in the society's treatment of the homeless. One of its special offshoot groups—the Committee on Special Relief—tended to the needs of the wealthier fire victims with great sympathy, noting these victims "were borne in a single night from homes of comfort and plenty into absolute destitution." This special committee figured that the well-to-do would have to be sought out because, it assumed, they would be too proud to ask for help. But members of the Relief and Aid Society believed that the homeless poor were a lower class, not worthy of the same compassion. The barracks provided adequate housing for this class, according to the society, which also believed the city would be best served by removing them from relief as quickly as possible. The society claimed it would give "no aid to any families who are capable of earning their own support."

To receive relief, applicants had to fill out forms and give a reference, preferably the name of a member of the clergy or an employer. A member of the society would then personally follow up on the request. Depending on who reviewed the case, the decisions about who should receive aid were quite subjective and not always fair. But by and large, the Chicago Relief and Aid Society provided much-needed aid to the devastated city and did so quite effectively.

Mayor Mason's term of office expired soon after the Great Fire, and in the November 1871 election Chicagoans voted *Tribune* co-owner Joseph Medill in as the new mayor. Medill had run on the Fireproof Party ticket and had pledged to pass stricter building codes.

Soon afterward the Chicago Common Council proposed establishing stricter antifire building regulations, which would require the use of brick or stone for any new buildings constructed in the Burnt District. Of course only the rich, who most likely had cashed in working fire insurance policies, could afford these fireproof materials. On January 15, 1872, a group of demonstrators, armed with signs that read "Leave a Home for the Laborer" and "Don't Vote Any More for the Poor Man's Oppressor," staged a nighttime march to protest the new and expensive building codes. Protesters drew up a petition stating that the proposed ordinance discouraged members of the working class from building private homes, because the only material they could afford was wood. The antifire legislation passed nonetheless. As a result, many poorer citizens moved out of the area, crowding into parts of the South and West Divisions, which did not have such restrictions.

Ironically, with the haste to rebuild, most of the new buildings were really no more fireproof than their predecessors had been. Often new buildings were under construction before the architects had finished drawing up blueprints. Wood was still largely substituted for stone, and buildings were still embellished with wooden ornaments, awnings, and cornices. And thanks to ineffective building inspections, the poor also managed to continue building homes of highly flammable wood.

The Great Rebuilding did include the construction of numerous fireproof structures. By 1872, Chicago boasted almost 20 miles of stone and brick structures, along with tens of thousands of smaller buildings either completed or well under way.

Still, in the midst of rebuilding, Chicagoans needed to make sense of the chaos caused by the fire. How did it start? Why did it blaze out of control? For the bewildered Chicagoans it was not enough to say the blaze was caused accidentally and then quickly spread because of strong southwesterly winds. An official investigation of the cause of the fire was made, while the citizens traded rumors and opinions.

Just hours after the fire started, a rumor had quickly spread that the blaze had been caused by Catherine O'Leary's cow. According to the story, Mrs. O'Leary, holding a kerosene lamp to light her way, had gone to the barn behind her house to milk one of her cows. After she set the lamp on the ground, the cow kicked it over, igniting the hay on the barn floor and starting one of the country's worst disasters. In its Monday, one-page edition, printed while the fire was still burning, the *Chicago Evening Journal* had published that very account.

No one was ever able to prove this story true. The two-week official inquiry made by the board of police and fire commissioners found Mrs. O'Leary innocent, noting that she and the rest of her family were in bed when the fire started. However, the *Journal* never retracted its version, and newspapers around the country soon repeated the story as the truth. Even though Chicago newspapers had no evidence to support this claim, Mrs. O'Leary—and her cow—became the scapegoat.

But others received blame as well. The rich pointed their fingers at the poor, asserting that their poorly constructed wooden homes acted as effective kindling for the Great Fire. The poor blamed the rich, stating that even though the well-to-do had enough money to construct truly fireproof buildings in the business district, they had failed to do so.

Still others found fault with the firemen who had fought so valiantly to tame the wild blaze. In Alfred Sewell's account of the fire, entitled *The Great Calamity! Scenes, Incidents and Lessons of the Great Chicago Fire of the 8th and 9th of October, 1871*, he disparaged chief fire marshal Robert Williams as "confused, bewildered, and utterly lost to usefulness." Sewell claimed that many of the firefighters were "in a condition of 'demoralization' that was painful and sad to witness. . . . Adding to their fatigue, many of the firemen indulged freely on Sunday in the use of intoxicating liquors. . . . A drunken Fire Department is . . . responsible for the destruction of Chicago."

While it is probably true that some of the firemen did indulge in a few drinks after the fire, Sewell's tone is unfair. He does not point out that some of these slow-moving, clumsy firemen had been up the night before, fighting the Saturday-night Canal Street blaze. They were exhausted and overworked. Many had not had time to rest, continuing to work despite smoke-congested lungs and blistered skin. Williams and his firemen had probably done the best job that they could in battling the blaze. But unfortunately Sewell's unjust labels stuck, and like Mrs. O'Leary, members of the fire department were blamed for the Great Chicago Fire and regarded with disdain for many years to come.

While much had been lost in the Great Fire, some people found a way to make a profit from the

(continued on p. 88)

WAS MRS. O'LEARY'S COW REALLY A SCAPEGOAT?

> Late one night, when we were all in bed
> Mrs. O'Leary lit a lantern in the shed.
> Her cow kicked it over,
> Then winked her eye and said,
> "There'll be a hot time in the old town tonight!"
> —*popular song lyric*

Mention the Great Chicago Fire, and chances are somebody will bring up the story of Mrs. O'Leary's cow starting the blaze by knocking over a lantern in the barn. But did Mrs. O'Leary's cow get a bum rap?

Many historians say yes. They claim that not enough evidence exists to prove what started the infamous blaze. A recent theory championed by Richard F. Bales of the Chicago Title Insurance Company points to Daniel "Peg Leg" Sullivan, a one-legged carriage driver and neighbor of Mrs. O'Leary. Bales contends that Sullivan was in the barn lighting a lantern or smoking a pipe on the night of October 8. Records of the official board inquiry into the fire show that Sullivan had an awful lot to say about its origin. Bales thinks Sullivan might have been trying to cover up his own guilt in causing the fire.

Other theories as to the start of the blaze include boys sneaking a smoke, spontaneous combustion, and a fiery meteor that split into pieces as it fell to earth October 8. The last theory could explain the simultaneous occurrence of catastrophic fires in Chicago and the lumber town of Peshtigo, Wisconsin (which killed some 1,200 people), as well as a smaller fire in Michigan.

On the other hand, evidence does indeed show that the Chicago fire began in the O'Leary barn, where the family had recently gathered enough coal, wood shavings, and hay to see them and their livestock through the winter. These flammable items would certainly have served as sufficient kindling for the Great Fire. Some claim that on the morning of the fire Mrs. O'Leary told people she had been in the barn when one of her cows kicked over a lantern. But the official report of the board of police and fire commissioners remained inconclusive, stating, "Whether it originated from a spark blown from a chimney on that windy night or was set on fire by human agency, we are unable to determine." After the fire, curiosity seekers

Among the first to blame Mrs. O'Leary's cow for starting the Great Fire was the Chicago Evening Journal, *which printed the rumor in its one-page Monday edition, published while the fire still raged.*

claimed to have found the pieces of the lantern behind Mrs. O'Leary's cottage, which ironically managed to survive the disaster.

If it can't be proved, then why does everyone blame this disaster on Mrs. O'Leary's unfortunate bovine friend? Probably because it offers a logical cause for such a destructive, horrible catastrophe. As they stood amid the smoking embers of the city, victims of this blaze needed to know how and why it had happened before they could begin to put their lives back together. Unfortunately, their resolution came at a high price for Mrs. O'Leary. Blaming her simply fueled already negative anti-Catholic and anti-immigrant sentiments. She was depicted as a lazy, drunken old crone, even though she was in her early forties when the fire occurred and was an indisputably hardworking and sober woman.

Tired of being persecuted, Mrs. O'Leary and her family sold their property and left the neighborhood, but she continued to be harassed by reporters for the rest of her life. When she refused their interviews, they painted unflattering portraits of her in their articles, which perpetuated the poor-immigrant stereotype. Her husband, Patrick O'Leary, died in September 1894, and Catherine passed away the following year, in July.

(continued from p. 85)

misfortune. Young people dug into the mountains of debris, rubble, and bricks in search of souvenirs—candlesticks, melted fused silverware, and sooty dishes—to sell to tourists. Seeing their success, adults got into the business, too. Thomas Bryan, for example, purchased the remains of the 7,200-pound courthouse bell and sold it to H. S. Everett, who melted down the scrap and recast it into commemorative souvenirs. One of the most popular of these was a small working replica of the original courthouse

Merchants sell relics from the Great Fire at an open-air market.

bell that was accompanied by a certificate of authenticity signed by members of the Board of Public Works.

Others made a profit publishing quickly assembled accounts of the fire, many haphazardly told and ranging in quality and price from cheap paperbacks to elegant, hardbound leather volumes adorned with gilded lettering. Many of these histories were written by the journalists who had reported on the fire, and the publications included illustrations and often sensationalized and graphic eyewitness accounts.

Chicago's tragedy also served to inspire artists, writers, and musicians, who created commemorative books, poems, and songs. The Reverend E. P. Roe's *Barriers Burned Away* (1872) sold more than a million copies and became one of the most popular novels of the late 19th century. Several poets, including John Greenleaf Whittier, Bret Harte, and Julia Moore, responded to Chicago's destruction in verse. Composers like George F. Root and P. P. Bliss composed what were later called "fire hymns," which became anthems for the disaster-weary Chicagoans. The following chorus comes from Root's song "From the Ruins Our City Shall Rise":

> But see! the bright rift in the cloud
> And hear! the great voice from the shore
> Our city shall rise! yes she shall rise
> Queen of the west once more.

But with the Panic of 1873 the city's hopes for a quick rebirth abruptly ended. In September of that year the failure of a major New York bank, Jay Cooke and Company, set off what would become a lengthy national depression. By the end of 1873 Chicago's unemployed workers were staging rallies outside of the offices of the Relief and Aid Society, chanting, "Bread or death." They wanted the society to give whatever remained of the $5 million in contributions for Chicago relief back to the city, for distribution to the needy.

Harder times followed in July of 1874, when yet another major fire struck the city. Flames destroyed 800 buildings in about 30 square blocks. The blaze had originated in the 400 block of South Clark Street and progressed in the same northeasterly direction as had the Great Fire of 1871, to Michigan Avenue and Van Buren Street, destroying millions of dollars worth of structures.

During the six-year economic depression virtually no new buildings went up in Chicago, since no one had the money for new construction. Fortunately, during this time the city attempted to adopt stricter safety rules and make improvements to its fire department, mostly because insurers threatened to leave the city unless it adopted stricter building codes.

When it was time to rebuild important new structures, many architects with an eye to the future took part. They included William Le Baron Jenney, Louis Sullivan, Henry Hobson Richardson, Daniel Burnham, and John Root. A fire-resistant standard evolved as architects replaced wood frames with steel girders, constructed exteriors of brick or granite, and crafted buildings in straight, clean lines. This style of American architecture came to be known as the Chicago School—magnificent, simple buildings that were not only stately to look at but were also truly fireproof. Most of the new structures rose up to much greater heights than had their predecessors, as architects took advantage of the newly invented hydraulic elevator.

The Home Life Insurance Company Building, built in the 1880s by architect William Le Baron Jenney, has the straight, clean lines and a modern design reflective of the Chicago School of architecture. Many of the skyscrapers built in the new Chicago followed this style.

Burned-out areas of the city were redesigned in a grid plan that would both make it easier for people to make their way through the streets and simplify the firefighters' route toward any blaze. As the city itself was redesigned, city planners also included picturesque parks along the lake.

With the rebuilding, the structure of Chicago changed completely. Just before the fire, Chicago was a pedestrian's city. Most Chicagoans—people of all racial, ethnic, and socioeconomic backgrounds—lived in the business district in the center of the city. People walked to work at the nearby mills, warehouses, and foundries or to schools, churches, and saloons.

But under the city's new design, stores were clustered into specific neighborhoods, and the resulting business district moved southward, pushing the poorer inhabitants out of the area. Ten years later hardly anyone lived in the business district anymore. It had developed into the heart of the city as a shopping, business, and entertainment area. Factories relocated to cheaper, larger plots of land in the West Division and in new suburban industrial districts.

As people relied more heavily on mass transportation to bring them to jobs in the center of the city, the growing middle class moved farther away, building homes near the trolley and cable car stations. Since the poor could not afford the cost of mass transit, they lived where they could walk to work. The new Chicago became much more fragmented and sprawling. Still, the city boasted more potential than ever.

A poster advertising the World's Columbian Exposition in 1893. Chicago hosted the event not only to commemorate the 400th anniversary of Columbus's journey to the New World but also to show off the modern new city.

City of Opportunity

A fter the Great Fire, Chicagoans lived largely in the present. Although city officials originally planned to erect a monument to commemorate the fire, it was never finished. People, by and large, preferred to concentrate their energies on building a brighter, more modern Chicago rather than looking back with sentimentality at the city that existed before 1871.

The new Chicago rose up quickly. People all over the world were amazed by the citizens' resiliency. The rebuilt city seemed to hold great promise. Many of the slums, like the shantytown of Conley's Patch, had burned down and left plots of land ripe with opportunity. Lured by its bright potential, people from all over the country, and eventually the world, relocated to Chicago in search of a new life.

Chicagoans rebuilt their lost city so quickly and so efficiently that by 1890—only 19 years after the fire—its population had swelled to more than a million people. At the time, only New York had more inhabitants.

Even such a spectacular recovery couldn't replace the losses suffered in the Great Fire. As well documented as the fire itself was, it is interesting to note that a large chunk of individual history turned to ashes during those fateful days in October 1871. Because hundreds of thousands of birth, death, marriage, and school records were consumed in the fire, many families with ties to the city have had difficulty tracing their ancestry back to the 1870s or earlier.

FIRE PREVENTION WEEK

In 1896 the National Board of Fire Underwriters, an organization of the fire insurance industry, helped bring about the formation of a new group, the National Fire Protection Association (NFPA). This new organization established standards for equipment such as sprinklers, fire doors, and extinguishers—effective tools for firefighting and fire prevention. Years later, a subgroup from the NFPA, called the Fire Marshals Association of North America (FMANA), decided to take fire prevention efforts one step further. Its members proposed commemorating the 40th anniversary of the Great Chicago Fire by developing a program to educate the public about the importance of fire prevention efforts. FMANA proposed that the anniversary week of the Great Fire be set aside for this purpose.

It would not be until 1925 that President Calvin Coolidge proclaimed the first National Fire Prevention Week, to take place the week of October 4–10. In his address Coolidge noted that some 15,000 lives had been lost in fires during the previous year, 1924. He stated, "It is highly desirable that every effort be made to reform the conditions which have made possible so vast a destruction of the national wealth."

Today tens of thousands of fire safety proponents—professionals and volunteers—participate in the observance of National Fire Prevention Week, which

The passage of time helped most city residents recover from the Great Fire. After people began to get their lives back in order, they collected their thoughts and constructed their personal records of the event. For many survivors, the fire was the most traumatic event they had ever lived through, and they told their accounts again and again. Retelling the stories probably also helped many come to terms with the terror they had faced and the loss they had endured. "Every one of the 334,270 people in Chicago on those fateful days had a story to tell, and they never tired of telling it," said Harry A. Musham, author of the first well-documented account of the fire, *The Great Chicago Fire, October 8–10, 1871,*

is observed annually during the week of October 9, the day the Great Chicago Fire did its greatest damage. During the week educators teach people about fire safety and preparedness, especially in the event of home fires.

The organization teaches proven fire prevention measures, including the use of smoke detectors and fire extinguishers; the establishment of a home fire escape plan, with regular practice drills for evacuation; the installation of escape ladders; and the education of all family members about what to do in the event of a home fire. Firefighters emphasize that the more prepared people are, the quicker they can escape unharmed from a blaze.

From one of the nation's worst disasters came a program that has helped prevent countless additional injuries and deaths due to fire.

A Fire Prevention Week poster designed by Philip M. Kalas of Edison Regional Gifted Center, in Chicago, observes the 125th anniversary of the blaze that ravaged Chicago.

published in 1941.

People continued to record their stories—even decades after the blaze—for several reasons. Its historical significance was clear. In addition, the families and friends of the survivors demanded written accounts for future generations to read. But monetary incentives also tempted many would-be writers and artists. Newspapers, magazines, and contemporary historians sought out first-person accounts to print in their publications. Over the years many of the narratives were privately printed. The Chicago Historical Society solicited fire narratives until the 1940s. Its archives and library now include more than 150 documented personal accounts of the Great Chicago Fire.

By 1893 the city could proclaim itself recovered, and to prove its restoration, it hosted one of the world's most magnificent fairs, the World's Columbian Exposition. Although the official reason for the celebration was to commemorate the 400-year anniversary of Columbus's discovery of America, Chicago leaders had ulterior motives. In addition to bringing revenue into the city by persuading vacationers to visit, they wanted the celebration to show the world how quickly Chicago had rebuilt itself. City officials wanted the world to know that Chicago, with its modern buildings and "fresh start," was a city of progress and hope.

One special day held during the fair was called Chicago Day, held on October 9. It began with a grandiose evening celebration, complete with floats, music, and fireworks. Posters advertising the event portrayed Chicago as an attractive young woman wearing a breastplate emblazoned with Chicago's simple but powerful motto, "I will." Quite aptly, a phoenix perched on the crown of the emblem.

In 1921 the city observed the 50th anniversary of the fire with the "Chicago Fire Semi-Centennial Observance," held from October 3 to 9. Ironically, advertisements for the event barely even mentioned the fire, except to say that it was the point after which all of the rebuilding began. The Chicago Association of Commerce urged that every possible organization participate in the observance, and so a bevy of civic, commercial, educational, religious, social, and neighborhood associations banded together and arranged a plethora of activities.

The festivities included a grand opening ceremony held before an audience of 5,000; an "Americanization Demonstration" in Grant Park, where 6,500 people attended a rededication ceremony of Chicago and witnessed the naturalization of 648 new American citizens; and a variety of speeches and sermons. A few of the major highlights included the publication of an illustrated book on Chicago and the performance of a play that featured a 500-voice chorus and a 100-piece orchestra.

Many consider the Great Chicago Fire as the inspiration for numerous fire safety and prevention efforts that eventually developed in the United States. In 1873 the National Board of Fire Underwriters (NBFU) commissioned a study of Chicago; its subsequent report listed the city's many weaknesses in effective fire defense. City leaders quickly complied with most of the board's recommendations, which included the establishment of fire limits (in which special fire prevention and building code restrictions were implemented in the downtown business district), increased water supply facilities for both fire departments and communities, the establishment of a fire marshal's bureau, and improvements to eliminate hazardous conditions. The NBFU ultimately developed a grading system for use in evaluating fire departments and the needs of their communities.

The same year the National Board of Fire Underwriters made its study of Chicago, the National Association of Fire Engineers (later renamed the International Association of Fire Chiefs) was organized in Baltimore, Maryland. Fire chiefs from 50 major U.S. cities met, with the goal of developing improved fire prevention and firefighter protection techniques.

The Great Fire holds special significance for the people of Chicago, especially its fire department. After the disaster, city firefighters were determined to make the technology of fighting fires a priority. Members of the Chicago Fire Department can claim credit for many of the subsequent innovations in the field of firefighting, including the snorkel truck; the fireplug, or hydrant; and the collapsible fire escape. The fire pole was invented in 1874 by a Chicago fire captain as a way for the men to quickly make their way to the ground floor. Even the firefighter helmet was invented in Chicago.

In 1881 the Chicago Historical Society commemorated the Great Fire by placing a marble plaque at the home that had replaced the O'Learys' ramshackle cottage at 137 De Koven Street. And 80 years later the city chose to build the Chicago Fire Academy on that same block. An abstract sculpture of flames, created by Egon Weiner, stands before the building to memorialize the fire.

Today the mention of Chicago evokes images of lofty skyscrapers, numerous restaurants, and lakeshore beaches and parks, not a desolate, smoldering prairie plagued by a chaotic fire. Propelled by the famous gusts that gave the Windy City its nickname and that helped spread the devastating fire, kaleidoscopic sailboats flutter

The Chicago Fire Academy, located at the corner of Jefferson and De Koven Streets. A specially marked spot on the floor of the academy indicates the approximate site of the O'Leary barn, where the Great Fire of 1871 began.

on the waters of nearby Lake Michigan. Chicagoans enjoy long, ambling walks around the city's lush parks and wide boulevards. Home to some of the grandest buildings, museums, restaurants, theaters, and businesses in the country and the world, Chicago has become a bustling metropolis home to more than 7.5 million people. The city also boasts the country's busiest airport, O'Hare, which helps cement the city's continuing role as the crossroads of the East and West.

Most people consider Michigan Avenue as the jewel of modern Chicago. This major thoroughfare is near the Loop—Chicago's business district—so named because of

The only two public buildings to survive the Great Fire were the water tower and waterworks pumping station. Designated a historical landmark in 1971, the water tower still stands, a testament to the resilience of the city.

the loops of elevated train tracks surrounding it. Michigan Avenue is lined with grand, historic buildings on one side and a tract of lush Grant Park on the other, dotted with a few buildings.

To the north runs the Chicago River and across the waterway lies the famous Magnificent Mile, lined with some of the world's most exclusive stores, restaurants, and hotels. Standing proudly near the end of the Magnificent Mile is the Chicago Water Tower, one of the few buildings to have survived the Great Fire. Now dwarfed by surrounding skyscrapers, the water tower serves as a reminder of the city's resilience, a sentimental landmark that unites the old Chicago with the new.

The very fire that almost destroyed Chicago in 1871 has become a symbol of the city's unity. The Windy City's major-league soccer team is called the Chicago Fire, and its fan clubs have adopted names like the "Pyromaniacs" and the "Barn burners."

Indeed, from its disastrous fire Chicago has risen like a phoenix from the ashes and has firmly taken its place in history as one of America's greatest architectural showcases.

Chronology

Summer 1871	Chicago suffers one of its worst droughts
October 7, 1871	
10:00 P.M.	A large blaze breaks out on Chicago's West Side; firefighters spend the next 16 hours battling the fire
October 8, 1871	
8:45 P.M.	Flames are noticed in the O'Learys' barn at De Koven Street on Chicago's West Division
9:00 P.M.	A fire alarm is sent from Goll's Drugstore but not recorded at Cook County Courthouse, the city's central fire-alarm office
9:30 P.M.	Watchman Mathias Schaffer sounds an alarm but misjudges the location of the blaze
10:00 P.M.	Fire spreads north to the steeple of St. Paul's Church
11:30 P.M.	Fire jumps the south branch of the Chicago River and begins burning the South Division, including Parmelee's Stables and Conley's Patch
October 9, 1871	
2:20 A.M.	Cook County Courthouse and its warning bell are destroyed by fire
3:00 A.M.	City waterworks pumps cease operation, cutting off city water supply
6:00 A.M.	Mayor Roswell B. Mason sends telegrams requesting help from surrounding communities
Noon	North Division fires reach North Avenue
3:00 P.M.	Flames continue north; the mayor signs an emergency proclamation establishing temporary rules to prevent looting and chaos and appoints a relief committee to distribute food and shelter to needy

Chronology

5:00 P.M.	Chicago Avenue Bridge catches fire
11:00 P.M.	Steady rainfall extinguishes the Great Fire
October 13, 1871	Mason relinquishes the administration of the relief effort to the Chicago Relief and Aid Society
January 1872	The poor protest against the new fireproofing codes, claiming they can afford only wood for rebuilding, despite its flammability
January 1873	More than 20 miles of new brick and stone buildings grace Chicago's streets; an economic depression sparked by the collapse of Jay Cooke and Company, the New York bank, puts a temporary halt to most rebuilding
July 1874	Another great blaze destroys nearly 50 acres and 800 buildings in Chicago
May–November 1893	World's Columbian Exposition gives Chicago the opportunity to show off the splendor of its rebuilt neighborhoods
October 1921	A festival in Chicago commemorates the 50th anniversary of the fire
October 1925	Observation of first Fire Prevention Week, established during the anniversary week of the Great Chicago Fire

Catastrophic Fires in History

The Burning of Rome
Date: July 19–27, A.D. 64

Cause: Fire originated in shops located near the Circus Maximus, the site of Rome's chariot races, which also caught fire

Death toll: Estimated at several thousand

Numbers made homeless: Estimated at hundreds of thousands

Physical damage: 4 of the city's 14 districts were completely destroyed

The Great Fire of London
Dates: September 2–5, 1666

Cause: Fire in baker's shop spread by powerful winds

Death toll: Estimated at 6, most likely much higher

Number made homeless: 100,000 to 200,000

Physical damage: Destroyed almost 1 square mile (approximately 4/5 of city); 13,300 buildings

The Great Chicago Fire
Dates: October 8–10, 1871

Cause: Undetermined, although according to legend a cow kicked over a lantern, and its flame ignited a blaze that was quickly spread by strong winds

Death toll: 250 to 300

Number made homeless: 90,000 to 100,000

Physical damage: Destroyed 4 square miles (approximately 1/3 of city), or 17,500 buildings

The Peshtigo Forest Fire
Dates: October 8–9, 1871

Cause: Undetermined; lumber town of Peshtigo is set on fire by forest blaze

Death toll: 1,200

Number made homeless: unknown

Physical damage: Destroyed 2,400 square miles of Wisconsin woodlands

Catastrophic Fires in History

San Francisco Earthquake and Fire

> Dates: April 18–21, 1906
>
> Cause: A major earthquake knocked over cooking stoves and downed electrical wires, both of which ignited at least 50 small fires; the temblor also destroyed water mains, hindering firefighters efforts to keep the flames from spreading
>
> Death toll: Over 3,000
>
> Number made homeless: 225,000
>
> Physical damage: Destroyed 500 city blocks; more than 28,000 buildings

Great Kanto Earthquake and Fire (Tokyo and Yokohama, Japan)

> Dates: September 1, 1923
>
> Cause: A severe earthquake knocked coals from open charcoal braziers, setting thousands of Japanese homes ablaze and rupturing water mains
>
> Death toll: More than 100,000; 43,000 unaccounted for
>
> Number made homeless: 1.5 million
>
> Physical damage: Destroyed more than 300,000 buildings in Tokyo, 60,000 in Yokohama

Bibliography

Books and Periodicals

Anderson, Norman D., and Walter R. Brown. *Historical Catastrophes: Fires.* Reading, Mass.: Addison-Wesley, 1976.

Aylesworth, Thomas, and Virginia Aylesworth. *Chicago.* New York: Blackbirch Press, 1990.

Belleck, Pam. "Barn Door Reopened on Fire After Legend Has Escaped." *The New York Times.* 17 August 1997.

Greene, Laurence. *America Goes to Press: The News of Yesterday.* Indianapolis: Bobbs-Merrill Co., 1936.

Lowe, David, ed. *The Great Chicago Fire: In Eyewitness Accounts and 70 Contemporary Photographs and Illustrations.* New York: Dover Publications, 1979.

Miller, Donald L. *City of the Century: The Epic of Chicago and the Making of America.* New York: Simon and Schuster, 1996.

Murphy, Jim. *The Great Fire.* New York: Scholastic, 1995.

Pfeiffer, Christine. *Chicago.* Minneapolis, Minn.: Dillon Press, 1988.

Sawislak, Karen. "Relief, Aid, and Order: Class, Gender, and the Definition of Community in the Aftermath of Chicago's Great Fire." *Journal of Urban History.* November 1993. V20, p 3 (16).

Websites

Chicago Public Library Digital Collections: The Great Fire of 1871 and the Rise of a Modern City
http://www.chipublib.org/digital/lake/CFDFire.html

The Great Chicago Fire and the Web of Memory (by the Chicago Historical Society and Northwestern University)
http://www.chicagohs.org/fire/

Chicago's "Great Fire" spurred innovations, CNN Interactive, 9 October 1996
http://www.cnn.com/US/9610/09/chicago.fire/

Index

Index

Index

Picture Credits

A freelance writer, DYNISE BALCAVAGE is also the author of eight other books: *Ludwig van Beethoven, Steroids, The Federal Bureau of Investigation, Janis Joplin, Iowa, Gabrielle Reece, Philip Sheridan,* and *Saudi Arabia*. She also updated a book called *Culture Shock: Syria* after traveling extensively in that country.

Balcavage has also written many magazine articles, essays, poems, short stories, and book reviews. She occasionally does poetry readings and teaches writing classes in the Philadelphia area.

Balcavage has visited many foreign lands, including Jordan, Israel, Morocco, and Turkey and has spent a great deal of time in France. She earned a bachelor of fine arts degree in visual arts from Kutztown University and a master of arts degree in English from Beaver College. She lives in Philadelphia with her husband, cat, and two birds.

JILL McCAFFREY has served for four years as national chairman of the Armed Forces Emergency Services of the American Red Cross. Ms. McCaffrey also serves on the board of directors for Knollwood—the Army Distaff Hall. The former Jill Ann Faulkner, a Massachusetts native, is the wife of Barry R. McCaffrey, a member of President Bill Clinton's cabinet and director of the White House Office of National Drug Control Policy. The McCaffreys are the parents of three grown children: Sean, a major in the U.S. Army; Tara, an intensive care nurse and captain in the National Guard; and Amy, a seventh grade teacher. The McCaffreys also have two grandchildren, Michael and Jack.